VOL. 1

THINK ABOUT THAT FOR A MINUTE

KELLY K

THINK! *about that for a minute*

Published by Kelly K Ministries
PO Box 1112 Kingfisher OK 73750

Front cover design by Ian Lundin
www.CXXIIapparel.com
Book design copyright © 2023 by Kelly K. Ministries All rights reserved.
Published in the United States of America

---

www.KellyKMinistries.com

ISBN: 9798373397520

DEDICATION

THIS BOOK IS DEDICATED TO MY MOM ECHO. I KNOW WHAT THE LOVE OF JESUS IS BECAUSE OF YOU. THANK YOU FOR BEING THE GREATEST EXAMPLE OF WHAT A JESUS FOLLOWER ACTUALLY LOOKS LIKE. I MISS YOU EVERY SINGLE DAY.

ENDORSEMENTS

Kelly K is witty & funny and makes THE WORD applicable to everyone where they are in their walk with Christ. His analogies are thought provoking. My viewers and I have thoroughly enjoyed our Monday morning devotionals and they continue to ask for more. Kelly K is changing lives with his clear delivery of The Gospel.

- Trisha Marroquí
  INFLUENCER
  @TikTokMomma7

If, your idea of growing closer to God should be boring, I encourage you to put this book down. This book is perfect for anyone wanting to enjoy getting to know Jesus more. Kelly K will challenge you through stories and prayers, making God's word leap from the pages into your life.

-Tom Coverly
 Speaker/TV HOST
@TomCoverlyTour

ENDORSEMENTS

Pastor Kelly K has penned a fantastic resource that's sure to challenge and strengthen your faith. This 40 day devotional is packed with practical insight, as well as unique perspectives full of wisdom. A wonderful tool you're sure to enjoy.

- Pastor Michael Rowan
  PASTOR/INFLUENCER
   @RevMichaelRowan

Are you tired of uninspiring, boring devotionals that you forget about 10 minutes after you walk out the door each morning? Kelly K is changing the game with this inspiring, eye-opening, life changing Book! It challenges you in your daily walk with Christ! Highly recommended!

-Blake Martin
INFLUENCER
@Blake_Speaks_Fire

ACKNOWLEDGMENTS

Lindsay, Brennen, Chase, Avery, Jaxx, and Jett - I love you all so much its ridiculous! This family is the greatest gift from God I have ever been given!Each of you make me a better person every day. Thank you for laughing at my "dad jokes" even though I KNOW you don't think they're funny. And thank you all for letting me use you in SO many sermon illustrations! Sorry I forgot to ask first....

Harlan and Susan Robertson- I don't know how to thank the 2 of you enough. You are my prayer warriors. You have single handedly kept this ministry going more times than I can count. This book would not be possible without you. Im honored God put you in my life. I pray for you every single day. I love you both.

Ian Lundin - Bro! This book cover and back is insane! I love it! You knocked it out of the park AGAIN! Thank you for being so amazing to work with. And even more than that, thank you for being such an amazing friend! Love you dude!

Heather Kughn - Girl, you're awesome! You took on the task of helping me with this book without the blink of an eye! I owe you one big time! THANK YOU! Now please stop commenting on social media about my Jncos, goth days, and "Officer Kopp" nickname! Just cause you've known me for 30+ years doesn't mean you gotta tell all my secrets! Love you!

LETTER TO THE READER

Dear Reader,

First I want to thank you for trusting me with teaching you the Bible. That is a great honor that I don't take lightly. The purpose of this devotional is to HELP you develop a stronger walk with God. Reading the Bible and letting His word touch your heart is such an important step in our daily lives, yet so many people (even Christians) skip it, miss it, or don't even care about it at all. Going to Church and going to Bible studies is fantastic. But nothing can compare to getting a revelation from the Lord yourself! This book is meant to help you build that habit in your life. The first 40 days is on me! The rest of your life, well… that's on you! This book doesn't have to be read in order. It doesn't have to be done every day. Take it at your own speed and pace. None of them should take you more than 5 minutes to read. That way there is no excuse for missing your time in HIS word. I hope this book blesses you. I hope you love every single day. But more importantly, I hope it stirs a hunger in you to get into God's Word for yourself! I promise you won't regret it!

Love,

Kelly K

1. LIKE, COMMENT, SHARE

Psalms 1:1-3

Oh, the joys of those who do not follow the advice of the wicked, or stand around with sinners, or join in with mockers. *But they delight in the law of the Lord,* meditating on it day and night. *They are like trees planted along the riverbank,* bearing fruit each season. Their leaves never wither, and they prosper in all they do.

THINK ABOUT THAT FOR A MINUTE

Have you ever seen those posts on social media that show a big pile of cash and read, "Like, comment, and share this post to receive your blessing?" If you have, you may have also noticed the thousands of likes, comments, and shares that they have. Those posts have always made me laugh. If it were that easy to be blessed by God, we would all be constantly liking, commenting, and sharing posts about huge stacks of cash! I actually even tried sharing one of those once. I never got my cash though . . . maybe my check was lost in the mail? But what if it WAS that easy? What if being blessed by God was actually a three-step process that was as easy as, "Like, Share, Comment?" Would you try it? Of course you would! So I have good news for you! IT IS THAT

EASY! There is a three step process. Our scripture today, and this entire book, is exactly that. Psalms 1 is essentially saying that those who love to read God's Word (the Bible) and think about it every day and night, will be blessed in ALL they do. Did you catch that? In ALL you do! This is simple. It doesn't say, read the whole Bible, memorize it, quote it out loud everyday, and THEN you will be blessed. It is as easy as reading a scripture every day and thinking about it throughout your day. That is the design and purpose of the very book you are about to read, to give you a scripture each day and then you just think about it throughout your day. Steps one and two of this process are on you, but step three, prosper in all you do, that's on God! And that's a promise from Him if you just follow steps one and two. You see, it says that if you do this, you will be like a tree that bears fruit in EVERY season. The crazy thing about that is, that's not normal for a tree to do! Leaves change in the fall, die in the winter, start to come back in spring and then are full and bright in summer. Notice, this didn't say every season would now be summer. In *every* season, you will prosper. You will still have winter seasons, when things seem cold and difficult, but it won't stop the blessings of God in your life. How amazing is that?!? Does it sound too good to be true? Have you ever liked, commented on, or shared one of those money posts? Then I guess forty days in this book, thinking about a scripture each day, is worth a try too!

LET ME CHALLENGE YOU TODAY

Set a goal for today that for the next forty days you'll meditate on the daily scripture. Simply put, read it, and just think about it. As much as we would like to think we read the Bible, the Bible will actually *read* YOU! If you will set this goal and stick with it, I will give you not only my word, but the promise of GOD, you *will* see your life start to prosper in all you do. This book will give you a scripture each day. *Or find one on your own.* This is just a guide to help. But don't be surprised when the verse for the next day in this book seems to be exactly what you need that day. God is good like that! Try it, I DARE you!

LET ME PRAY FOR YOU TODAY

God, we thank You today for Your Word and Your promises to us! We are so grateful that You not only showed mercy on us by sending Your Son to pay for our sins, but that You also extended to us grace, with blessings that we may not deserve, but You promised them to us anyway. God, give us a hunger for Your Word today. Give us a passion and desire to read and meditate on at least one scripture every day. And we thank You for honoring Your promise to us by blessing us in EVERY season of our lives! We are excited to see what YOU can do through us over the next forty days. In Jesus' name, Amen.

What is God speaking to you today?

_____

_____

_____

_____

_____

_____

_____

_____

_____

_____

_____

_____

_____

_____

_____

_____

_____

_____

_____

_____

_____

_____

_____

_____

_____

2. FLIP TO THE B-SIDE

John 4:28

The woman left her water jar beside the well and ran back to the village telling everyone.

THINK ABOUT THAT FOR A MINUTE

When you were a kid, did you have a plan for what you wanted to be when you grew up? Does your life now look exactly like what you had PLANNED it to be all those years ago? At one point I was hoping to be a famous rapper. You can see how well that worked out for me . . . We all have plans, an idea of how we expect our life to go, some direction or purpose we decide to pursue. But what if our plan doesn't match God's plan for us? One thing I have definitely learned in all my time as a Christian is that my plan and God's plan almost never look the same. In our scripture today we read just one short line out of the story of the woman at the well. *(If you have time today, read the whole story. You won't be disappointed!)* You see, when she woke up that day she had a plan to avoid everyone and get water at noon because everyone else got water in the morning. She was planning to get water and go back home to finish out the rest of her plans for the day. The funny thing is, after having an encounter with Jesus, she ends up leaving her jar beside the well. Not only that, but now she is looking for the same people that only moments ago she wanted to avoid. Does this strike you as odd? It doesn't to me. Scripture also tells us, "His thoughts are not our thoughts, and His ways are not our ways" (*Isaiah 55:8*) When I was growing up I had to listen to music on a cassette. If you're too young to know what that is, good for you! Google it. A cassette, for those who were fortunate enough to experience it, had an A-side and a B-side. The A-side is where the artist, management, and record label would put the songs that THEY thought were going to be the biggest hits. That's because people normally listened to the A-side first. However sometimes the songs that were placed on the B-side actually turned out to be bigger hits than any of those on the A-side. You see this woman came to the well on her A-side. Her OWN plan for her life. But after an encounter with Jesus, she flips to the B-Side! She came wanting water but left her jar beside the well. Despite going at noon to avoid people, she left looking for everyone. We all have a plan that we think is perfect for our lives, one that will be a *hit*. But if we just let Jesus flip us to the B-Side there may be bigger hits in store for us than we ever could have planned on our own!

LET ME CHALLENGE YOU TODAY

Evaluate the plans that you have made for your life today. Are you frustrated that things haven't worked out the way you wanted? Are you willing to let Jesus into the middle of your plans? Even if that means flipping to the B-Side and trying something new? Take time today to ASK God what He wants for your life. And then take time to get quiet and listen. Your greatest hit may be closer than you think!

LET ME PRAY FOR YOU TODAY

Jesus, we thank You that You always take time to meet us right where we are. We thank You for the gifts, talents, and abilities You have given us. And now God, we are asking that You show us what YOUR plan is for us. We want to know how to use what You gave us to not only *better* our own life, but also so that You get the glory for all of it! Flip us to the B-side today Jesus! We want to encounter You in such a new way today that we can't wait to run and tell everyone what You are doing in our lives! We thank You for all You are doing in us today as we offer to lay our plans beside the well. We love You and honor You today, in Jesus' name. Amen.

What is God speaking to you today?

_____

_____

_____

_____

_____

_____

_____

_____

_____

_____

_____

_____

_____

_____

_____

_____

_____

_____

_____

_____

_____

_____

_____

_____

3. DON'T BELIEVE IN GHOSTS

Mark 6:49:50

But when they saw him walking on the water, they cried out in terror, thinking he was a ghost. They were all terrified when they saw him.
But Jesus spoke to them at once. "Don't be afraid," he said. "Take courage! I am here!"

THINK ABOUT THAT FOR A MINUTE

Have you ever seen a ghost? Neither have I. Now, there may be a select few who have *'ghost stories'* but I can only imagine that's exactly what they are. Stories. In our scripture today we find the disciples out on a lake and struggling for their lives in the middle of a horrible storm. But have no fear, right? Jesus sees them and He's coming to help! However, as soon as He approaches by walking on the water, their first thought is, "This MUST be a ghost!" Again, let me ask, have you ever witnessed a ghost? Well I would be willing to bet anything that the disciples never had either. Now don't get me wrong, these boys have seen Jesus cast out demons on MANY occasions. They know demons are real and have seen what that looks like, but they didn't say they thought they saw a "demon." They said it was a ghost. They said, "Patrick Swayze!", I mean, "GHOST!" *(hahaha)* When I first read this I laughed, thinking, *"These guys hang out with Jesus everyday! He does miracles and extraordinary things every single day! Extraordinary should be ordinary for these guys at this point! Right?" Why would they not just KNOW this is Jesus?"* I laughed. Until I realized this is the same thing you and I do all the time. We have seen Jesus work in our lives. We have seen Him show up in the most difficult of times. We can recall multiple times when He has come to our rescue. We know He is always with us and we know He is our anchor in every storm. We know all of this, but how is it so often that Jesus is the last thing we think of when things start to turn wrong or get difficult in our lives? Sometimes it seems like *"believing in ghosts"* is a better option than believing in Jesus. It can seem like a better idea to get advice from other sources before turning to the Word of God. It can be easier to panic and try to borrow money for an unexpected bill before praying and asking God for help or for wisdom. It's even easier to believe the worst instead of casting all your fears, cares, and worries on Christ. Do you believe in ghosts? I don't either. But Jesus says, "Don't be afraid, take courage! I am here!" and *that*, I do believe.

LET ME CHALLENGE YOU TODAY

Make a choice today to turn to Jesus FIRST. Believe His Word first. Whatever storm you're struggling through, whatever problem, fear, or worry is weighing you down, decide right now that Jesus is *the* answer and not a last-ditch option. Take your problem to Him and stand on His Word. Don't be afraid! Take courage! HE IS WITH YOU!

LET ME PRAY FOR YOU TODAY

Jesus, I thank You that You see us in the middle of our storms. I thank You that your Word promises us You will never leave us or forsake us. Today I pray that as each reader thinks about this scripture, that You will renew their faith in You, to believe that You are the best option, the first option, and the only option for their life! We give our fear, doubt, and worry to You today, Jesus. We choose to take courage, stand in faith, and know that You are right here in the middle of the storm with us. Thank You for renewing our faith in You today. In Jesus' Name, Amen.

What is God speaking to you today?

_____

_____

_____

_____

_____

_____

_____

_____

_____

_____

_____

_____

_____

_____

_____

_____

_____

_____

_____

_____

_____

_____

_____

4. OH FOR SHAME

Mark 14:49-52 NLT

"Why didn't you arrest me in the Temple? I was there among you teaching every day. But these things are happening to fulfill what the Scriptures say about me." Then all his disciples deserted him and ran away. One young man following behind was clothed only in a long linen shirt. When the mob tried to grab him, he slipped out of his shirt and ran away naked."

THINK ABOUT THAT FOR A MINUTE

Can you think of a moment in your life that you were so absolutely embarrassed by that you NEVER wanted to let anyone know it happened? Of course you can! We all can. I spoke at a church in San Antonio a few years ago. They had me as a guest speaker and another guy I hadn't met or heard of before. We were both staying at the same hotel and the church asked if I could give this guy a ride since he had flown in and I drove. I told them that it was no problem! As we're driving, he points out a motorcycle and says, "That guy is wearing a Mongols vest." I then proceeded to share with him all I knew about the Mongols gang, making sure he knew that I knew how bad those guys were! He let me talk for at least

16

fifteen minutes before he finally told me that he started that gang. Turns out I was sitting next to *Big Al Aceves*, founder of the Mongols. One of the baddest dudes in the history of bad dudes! Luckily for me, Jesus had changed his life! I was SO embarrassed. Those moments in life are painful. We just want them to go away forever, am I right? So in today's scripture we find in Mark's Gospel that Jesus is being arrested in the garden of Gethsemane. Now this would have been a traumatic moment. Guards show up out of nowhere, Jesus' friend sells him out, the Roman guards are putting their hands on Jesus to restrain Him . . . you can imagine it like a scene from a movie but Jesus isn't fighting back. In fact, He said that all these things were happening to fulfill scripture. Then we read the unthinkable. His disciples deserted Him. They all ran away, scared for their own lives. If I was Mark and writing this account *and I had to tell the truth*, that I ran away and deserted Jesus, this may be one of the most shameful moments of my life. I bet it stung just to have to write that book. But wait! It keeps coming! Mark then tells us about a young man who was in his jammies when they tried to grab him. He ended up running away from the scene completely buck naked! When I first read that I laughed to myself and thought, "why is that in the Bible?" Have you ever had that thought about something you read? Well here is what I know, everything that is in the Bible is there with a purpose, to teach us something. OK Mark, so why are you telling us about this guy? As I dug into different commentaries to learn about this passage, I found out that most scholars believe that Mark is retelling this story about HIMSELF! Mark reveals this super embarrassing moment to us, forever recorded in scripture for the rest of eternity! WHY?! I believe this verse is here to teach us, No matter what we have lived through, no matter how shameful our past may be, God still desires to use those moments to bring glory to His name. He doesn't only want to use your "amazing "moments. He wants to use your shame too. If you let Him. Your shameful past may be the key someone else needs to unlock their future with Christ. Be open & be willing to share and see how God will use even your lowest to reveal His glory!

LET ME CHALLENGE YOU TODAY

Today take some time and think about those moments in your life that you have been ashamed of and remind yourself, "There is no condemnation in Christ Jesus" (Romans 8:1). Remind yourself, Jesus is NOT ashamed of you. You don't have to be either. If those moments still cause a slight sting, allow God to begin healing those wounds. Ask Him how He can allow you to use those hurts to bring glory to His name! There is nothing better than watching God use for His glory what the enemy tried to use to destroy you!

LET ME PRAY FOR YOU TODAY

Jesus, thank You for not being ashamed of us today! Thank You for knowing us completely and loving us anyway. We give You all of our past hurts, disappointments, and shameful moments. We ask You to completely remove all shame from our lives and heal any open wounds we may still have. God, please show us, and open doors for us to use these moments to bring You glory! We thank You that the enemy has already been defeated and what he tried to use to harm us, You will turn around and use for good. Thank You for using every part of us today! In Jesus' name. Amen.

What is God speaking to you today?

_____

_____

_____

_____

_____

_____

_____

_____

_____

5. F.E.A.R

Psalms 25:14 NLT

The Lord is a friend to those who fear him. He teaches them his covenant.

THINK ABOUT THAT FOR A MINUTE

Did you ever have a coach or a parent that ever tried to motivate you with the phrase, "I'll put the fear of the Lord in you!" Oh man, I sure did! That phrase still gives me goosebumps to this day, normally because a spanking, or some form of punishment followed right after it. So that was always weird for me when studying the Bible, because all throughout scripture we see this term used, "Fear the Lord." and we read so many promises that come with fearing the Lord, such as, *you'll be a friend* of God, He will tell you His secrets, *You will be abundantly blessed, G*od will honor you, and so m*any more.* But hold on... Isn't "fear" the total opposite of God? This can be extremely confusing. The Bible says, "Perfect love casts out all fear." (1 John 4:18) But then the Bible also says, "The Lord is a friend to those who fear Him." So....? Are you confused yet? I sure was! That is, until I started looking at it in a different way. Fear, if we break it down, will stand for, "Forget Everything And Run." Because that's what we do most of the time when we are afraid. We forget who we are and where we are. We forget everything and we just run. The key to understanding here is that the sentence isn't complete yet! To finish the sentence we need to know where you're running to! You can forget everything and run AWAY *or* you can forget everything and run TO GOD! So really it is just all about HOW you finish that sentence! Serving God out of fear of what will happen to you if you don't will only carry you so far before you burn out. I hate that so many Christians try to live this way. "I'm afraid of going to hell, so I will try and serve God and do the right things." That's why we see so many burnt out believers. It breaks my heart. However, serving God because you are so afraid of what life would be like AWAY from Him... *that* is true love! And that makes you a friend of God. We don't need to be terrified of WHO God is. He loves us! He is not just a "get out of hell" ticket. We need to be afraid of a life WITHOUT Him, without His love. To me, THAT is the only truly terrifying thing that exists.

LET ME CHALLENGE YOU TODAY

Examine for yourself what it looks like to "Fear the Lord." Is that a phrase that brings up bad feelings or good feelings? Take some time today to search out a few scriptures and see what God says about those who fear Him. Ask God today to reveal to you exactly what that phrase means. And ask Him to give you a genuine fear of the Lord. I promise you, this won't be something scary, but one of the most beautiful and freeing revelations you will ever discover. Seriously, give it a try!

LET ME PRAY FOR YOU TODAY

Father, thank You for being such a loving and kind God! We thank You that we don't have to be afraid of You. We don't have to be afraid of disappointing you. God, I ask You today to give us a fresh revelation of what it truly means to fear the Lord. God, give us a hunger and a desire for You like never before and to truly fear any life we could ever live that didn't have You in it! Thank You for all the wonderful promises You give us once we understand how to truly fear You! In the mighty name of Jesus, we receive them all today. Amen.

What is God speaking to you today?

_____

_____

_____

_____

_____

_____

_____

_____

_____

_____

_____

_____

_____

_____

_____

_____

_____

_____

_____

_____

_____

_____

_____

_____

6. THE GREAT BACON PLUNGE

MARK 5:12-13

"Send us into those pigs," the spirits begged. "Let us enter them." So Jesus gave them permission. The evil spirits came out of the man and entered the pigs, and the entire herd of about 2,000 pigs plunged down the steep hillside into the lake and drowned in the water.

THINK ABOUT THAT FOR A MINUTE

I think one of the greatest tragedies in our world today is that we have to ASK to add bacon to our burgers. Seriously, don't make me ask, just assume I want it there! What is better than a bacon burger, am I right? I don't even mind that you're planning to charge me for it, I'm prepared to ask for it anyway! Here's what's really crazy though, I know adding bacon to my burger is going to cost me something, but that doesn't make me afraid to ask for it. But when it comes to God, our Father, how many times do we simply not even ask Him for what we need even when there is *no* cost involved at all? God's Word tells us over and over to present our requests to Him, to come BOLDLY before His throne, and to ask for ANYTHING in His name and He will do it. *But we don't.* So many times we complain about our issues to our friends, post them on social media, or just dwell on them instead of taking them to God. Why not? I think most of the time, if we are honest about it, we feel unworthy. We know who we really are deep down. We know the mistakes we make each day. We know our failures. We know these things and for some reason we think that makes us "less" in the eyes of God. Why would God want to bless ME? Answer a prayer for ME? Give good gifts to ME? Have you ever felt that way? I know I have. Let's look at today's extremely *strange* scripture though. In this story here, Jesus is about to cast out a "legion" of demons from a man that was so possessed that the town he lived in actually chained him up in the cemetery *(and you thought YOU had it bad)*. Jesus showed up at this cemetery, of course He was there to heal this man, but pay attention to what was happening. Before Jesus commanded the demons to leave, they asked Jesus for a favor, to be sent into a herd of pigs. Who asked? *They.* The DEMONS. Not the man! Catch this, these were demons asking the Son of GOD for a favor! At first glance at this, I was thinking, "How crazy and stupid are you demons? There is NO WAY Jesus would ever answer a request from you!" but that's not what happens at all, is it? The scripture says, "So Jesus gave them permission." Jesus, the Son of God, just answered the request of a demon. Wow. I don't care how unworthy, how wrong, or sinful you may feel your life is, I guarantee you don't even come CLOSE to a demon. That's what I want you to take away from this verse today. If Jesus will answer the prayer of a demon, how much more so will He take joy in answering a request for you? The demons, who hated God, wanted some bacon and He let them have it. You are His child and He loves more than anything. Don't be afraid to go boldly, with confidence, before Him and present your requests to God.

LET ME CHALLENGE YOU TODAY

Today, take your requests to God. No matter the size, tell God what you need. Go to Him with the confidence that He is your Father and He loves you more than anything. Go with full expectation that God not only hears you, but He WANTS to give you the desires of your heart. You are so much more valuable than any demon. You are the righteousness of Christ and it brings joy to the Father when you bring Him your requests.

LET ME PRAY FOR YOU TODAY

God, we thank you so much today for your love that is not based on what we do but on who we are to You. Renew our minds today, let us see ourselves the way You see us. So that we can have the confidence to bring You anything and everything. You are our loving Father who wants to be involved in every decision, process, and moment in our lives. Thank You for Your promises and for reassuring us over and over in Your Word that we can come to You with anything. Forgive us for ever trying to keep things from You. Today we gladly bring You our requests. In Jesus' name, Amen.

What is God speaking to you today?

_____

_____

_____

_____

_____

_____

_____

_____

_____

_____

7. SHEEP NEED A SHEPHERD

Psalms 23:1

The Lord is my shepherd; I shall not want.

THINK ABOUT THAT FOR A MINUTE

Can I be honest with you for a minute? When I was really digging into the Bible for the first time, I was annoyed with how many times the Bible referred to me as a SHEEP. I understand that was common language back then and people understood the imagery because being a shepherd was a common occupation. But come on man! If the Word of God has to refer to me as an animal, can't it at least be a COOL one? Can't I be compared to a cobra or a liger? Anything but sheep! I truly felt this way. I know this sounds completely ridiculous too, but as a Christian I want to be compared to something powerful. With Jesus I know I can accomplish anything but what has a sheep ever accomplished? Nothing. So in my mind this is a *Baaaaaaa-d* comparison. *(Dad Joke. You're welcome)* I *WAS* annoyed. I'm not anymore. That's because God showed me the "why" behind the importance of us being sheep. It's not even so important that we are the sheep, the importance is that HE is our SHEPHERD. Here is what God revealed to me. If you were to embark on a long ride out in a beautiful Oklahoma pasture, would you choose to ride a sheep? No. If you were going to hike a trail and you needed an animal to carry all of your camping gear up the mountain, would you choose a sheep? No. Why not? Because sheep are not load-bearing animals. THEY ARE NOT MADE TO CARRY ANY WEIGHT. In that sentence right there everything became completely clear to me. Sheep were not designed to carry anything. That is a shepherd's job! Sheep NEED a shepherd because they do not have the ability to handle life on their own. And neither do we. When a sheep has a good, trustworthy shepherd that takes care of them and protects them then they don't need anything else. They carry no stress, no worry, and no anxiety. They can rely and trust fully that their shepherd will protect them and provide for all of their needs. You have the greatest *Shepherd* of all time! Our verse today says that the Lord is YOUR *Shepherd*, and that means everything is taken care of! This is great news! You don't have to carry one worry, not one stress, around with you today. As soon as you feel the weight of your job, family, finances, friends, health, or whatever it may be weighing you down, just remember that you were not made to carry any weight! You can truly let go and give that all to your Shepherd. The problem is, when we try to take care of our issues on our own, we are actually preventing our Shepherd from doing His job. We are saying that we know better than Him and we can handle this on our own. The truth is that you can't. I can't. We were never supposed to be able to. Our job is to be loved, cared for, and protected. So don't try and lift what you were never meant to carry. Remember that the Lord is YOUR *Shepherd,* who will always and has always, provided for ALL of your needs. If you just let Him.

LET ME CHALLENGE YOU TODAY

Consider taking a closer look at your life today. Have you been carrying unnecessary weight? Do you live most days stressed out, worried, or depressed? Does it feel like you have needs that still need to be met? Today I challenge you to honestly let go of the things that are weighing you down and give them to the Lord, your *Shepherd.* Trust that He is the "Good Shepherd" and He really does have your best interests in mind. Let Him carry the weight and just enjoy spending time in His presence!

LET ME PRAY FOR YOU TODAY

God, we thank You that YOU are our *Shepherd*. Thank You that we don't have to carry any of the weight this world tries to put on us. God, today as we start to feel weighed down with stress or anxiety, help us to remember that we can run to You and that Your burden is light. God may each reader physically feel lighter, even right now while saying this prayer, as You show them what a good *Shepherd* You are by removing any unnecessary burdens they may have been carrying for so many months or even years. Thank you Father, for Your love and peace that You give, that never weighs us down, but always lifts us up. In Jesus' name, Amen.

What is God speaking to you today?

_____

_____

_____

_____

_____

_____

_____

_____

8. PASS OR FAIL

James 4:17

Remember, it is sin to know what you ought to do and then not do it.

THINK ABOUT THAT FOR A MINUTE

High school was not my favorite thing to do growing up. Neither was elementary or middle school, in fact I was more of a class clown. I know, surprise, surprise! Honestly, I just hated tests. They stress me out! Reality is that we have to take tests our entire lives whether we like them or not. They may not be the same type of tests we take at school, but God is giving us tests each and every day. I guarantee you that we all can think of a time that we knew God was testing us. You remember? You felt it so clearly. You knew EXACTLY what God wanted you to do and you said, "No, God, I'll pass. I'll catch you on the next one. I'm not ready for this test today". Now don't beat yourself up too badly. I've been in that exact same position myself more than once.. This used to be a normal practice for me, hearing God but then ignoring God. So what does that mean exactly? Essentially what we're saying is that we know better than God. We hear what You are asking us to do

God, but we have a BETTER plan in mind. Ouch. That's not fun to hear. But we say this to God all the time with our ACTIONS. Honestly, I really did behave like this all the time until I realized something, your obedience to God may have nothing to do with you, but everything to do with someone else. Let that sink in. Your obedience to God may have *nothing* to do with you, but *everything* to do with someone else. What if the test God was giving you actually had nothing to do with you? Perhaps, what God is asking of you may not actually be a test at all? Someone else's blessing may be waiting on the other side of your obedience. Someone else's salvation may be hanging on the thread of YOUR obedience. You see, God uses the obedience of His people to bring peace, hope, love, blessings, and salvation into OTHER people's lives! Jesus said it was good that He was on earth but even better that He departed. When Jesus left the earth His ministry didn't end. He gave us the same Holy Spirit He had and He expects us to carry on the ministry where He left off. Jesus was only one *man*, but we are many! Imagine the possibilities! Don't fear the test, just look forward to it knowing someone's life is about to be changed forever! Even if it's yours.

LET ME CHALLENGE YOU TODAY

Let's change our mindset today. Let's start seeing obedience to God not as a test but as the miracle somebody else has been waiting for. I challenge you today to ask God to give you an opportunity to pass a test but understand what this means when you ask. It means He is going to test you! Be listening for God's voice today, and when He speaks, DO IT! Without delay! God has work to do and He wants to do it through YOU! There is nothing more satisfying than hearing God's voice and doing what He says. You may not always see the outcome of God's plan, but the overwhelming feeling of fulfillment you will have from obeying is reward enough. I promise!

LET ME PRAY FOR YOU TODAY

Lord, we thank You for the chance to be obedient to You today! God forgive us for the many times we've missed or ignored what You were asking us to do. Give us a chance to obey You today and we promise to obey without delay. God change our hearts about the way we respond to Your voice. May we be hungry and passionate to dive headfirst into whatever it may be You have for us. We trust in You and Your process. In Jesus' name, Amen.

What is God speaking to you today?

_____

_____

_____

_____

_____

_____

_____

_____

_____

_____

_____

_____

_____

_____

_____

_____

_____

_____

_____

_____

_____

9. ANCHORS AWAY

Hebrews 6:19

This hope is a strong and trustworthy anchor for our souls. It leads us through the curtain into God's inner sanctuary.

THINK ABOUT THAT FOR A MINUTE

Our scripture today is all about putting our hope and faith in Jesus. We LOVE this scripture don't we? I've seen this verse on T-shirts. I've seen so many anchor tattoos with this scripture reference. I've even seen it on bumper stickers! Look, I get it, anchors look cool and this verse makes anchors sound amazing. Until you need to use one. Have you ever thought about that? The way you use an anchor is in the middle of a storm. This is when your boat is being thrashed around, when the waves are out of control, and when your life is in danger. You throw it over the side so that it sinks to the bottom and holds you in place. Pay attention, an anchor HOLDS YOU THERE. Wait, so God's hope is so that we go through the storm? Yes. Absolutely. Let's be honest, what we really want this scripture to say is, "*This hope is a strong and trustworthy helicopter.*" That's what we really want isn't it? God, please fly in and get me out of here! But what He's telling us is, "I see you in the storm. I see your struggle. I see your tears. But I'm not taking you out of it. I'm going to hold you steady all the way THROUGH it." The thing we need to understand and remember is that it's the storms of life that build you into the person God has called you to be. If God pulled us out of the storm as soon as it started then we would never have a chance to develop our character fully. Storms aren't fun. Trust me, *I know*. But it should be extremely comforting to know that our hope and trust in Jesus is a strong, solid, trustworthy anchor. We may be going through a storm but we know we can have confidence that we won't be blown off course. We know we won't be destroyed. We know we're not alone! Our hope in Christ is like an anchor for our souls, providing stability, security, and access to God. As we deepen our relationship with Jesus and hold onto this hope, we can live as anchored people, even in the midst of life's storms. Let us continue to fix our eyes on Jesus, our forever *High Priest*, who has gone before us and made a way for us to REALLY know God.

LET ME CHALLENGE YOU TODAY

Let God truly be the anchor of your soul. Stop praying for a quick exit out of the storm that you're in. Hold on to Him and His Word because you're anchored in the promises of God. Change your perspective about the "storm" you may find yourself in today. See it as the situation that will bring about your elevation! Let God USE this time to build you, strengthen you, and develop you! He has NEVER left anyone out in the storm alone. He won't start today with you!

LET ME PRAY FOR YOU TODAY

God, we thank You today that You are our hope in the middle of the storm! God, change our minds today so that we don't focus on how bad things around us may seem. Let us instead focus on You. Thank You for USING this storm to build us and shape us into being more like You. Thank You for USING this storm as preparation for our elevation. We trust Your timing and Your process. Thank You that as we put our trust in You, You will lead us into Your inner sanctuary where we can experience the fullness of Your presence. In Jesus' name, Amen.

What is God speaking to you today?

_____

_____

_____

_____

_____

_____

_____

_____

_____

_____

_____

_____

_____

_____

_____

_____

_____

_____

_____

_____

_____

_____

10. "I WOULD NEVER DO THAT!"

MATTHEW 26:14-16

Then Judas Iscariot, one of the twelve disciples, went to the leading priests and asked, "How much will you pay me to betray Jesus to you?" And they gave him thirty pieces of silver. From that time on, Judas began looking for an opportunity to betray Jesus.

THINK ABOUT THAT FOR A MINUTE

Have you ever regretted a transaction you made? Maybe you sold something you couldn't replace or even made an unwise trade? I sure have. I remember collecting sports cards as a teenager. One of my all time favorites, which I was so proud of, was a Michael Jordan rookie card. I loved it so much! But then *RICKY!* I had an older friend named Ricky *(If you're reading this Ricky, I'm still mad!)* and he had a Topps Finest, Emmitt Smith, blue foil card! It was so pretty! This card would shine in the light when you moved it side to side. Oh boy did I want it! Ricky knew how badly I wanted it so when it came time to offer me a trade, you can only imagine what he asked for in trade; my Michael Jordan rookie card. Now this was at a time when the Dallas Cowboys were on top of the world! They were winning super bowls, they were unstoppable!

How could this be a bad trade, right? Well it was. I still own that Emmitt Smith card to this day. It is valued at $120. At the time I'm writing this, the Michael Jordan card is valued at $10,000. What a horrible transaction! Now, in our scripture today, Judas actually reached out and asked "How much will you pay me to betray Jesus?" He is making the worst trade of all time! They gave him 30 pieces of silver to sell out Jesus. That is equivalent to about $600 for us today. I think it goes without saying, but the question we all have is, *"HOW COULD YOU DO THAT?"* We would NEVER sell out Jesus for $600, right? Oh, really? The truth is, we sell out Jesus all the time. It may not be for money, but we actually do the exact same thing. We sell out Jesus for people, for relationships, for jobs, for websites we shouldn't be visiting, for alcohol, for drugs, or just for a moment of pleasure. We are constantly betraying Jesus because we think we can find something that can fulfill us better than He does. *At least Judas got $600,* all you got was an addiction and a guilty conscience. We sell out because we're looking for fulfillment, but all of those things only leave us more empty and void. The truth is that only Jesus gives you true fulfillment. The world is really good at marketing sin so that it looks like it will make you happy, and it might feel good for a brief moment in time, but it cannot leave you feeling fulfilled and satisfied. *Only Jesus can do that.* The question needs to be, "Is Jesus enough for me?" *Not if* Jesus is enough, but *is* He enough for *me*?

LET ME CHALLENGE YOU TODAY

Stop looking for bargains on your fulfillment. Jesus already paid it off. Don't sell out for something that's only going to leave you empty. Nothing is ever able to truly fill you up like Jesus will. Stop running to people, places, and things to give you what ONLY Jesus can. Take some time and examine your life today. What have you been "selling" Jesus for? Let Him know you recognize the mistake and make room for Him to bring you TRUE fulfillment today!

LET ME PRAY FOR YOU TODAY

Father, we thank You today! Thank You for paying the price for us. Forgive us for putting anything in our lives in place of You. God if we have sold you out for anything else to try to bring us happiness and fulfillment, please bring it to our attention so that we can invite You back into ALL areas of our lives. Thank You that You aren't mad at us when we miss it. Thank You for taking us back into Your arms and loving us even right now. Give us peace, joy, and Your perfect fulfillment today! You are worth it all! In Jesus name, Amen.

What is God speaking to you today?

11. THE KANSAS CITY SHUFFLE

MATTHEW 27:40

"Look at you now!" they yelled at him. "You said you were going to destroy the Temple and rebuild it in three days. Well then, if you are the Son of God, save yourself and come down from the cross!"

THINK ABOUT THAT FOR A MINUTE

I love playing games with my kids. God can teach you so much through children. My son, Jaxx, and I like to play a trading card game together called CUE. You collect the cards and then build decks to compete your cards against other players. Each card has a different power level and each card has a different ability. Some cards give you more strength when you're winning, but then there are some that work best when you're losing. There is a lesson in that. When I read today's scripture, it was so uplifting to me. Now, I know what you're thinking, that it doesn't seem uplifting AT ALL. But notice, this was yelled at Jesus while He was being crucified. What's so crazy to me is that He was LITERALLY in the middle of doing the very thing He was being accused of *not* doing! "You said you were going to destroy the Temple and rebuild it in three days!" they shouted. The problem here is, THEY were looking for the "temple" as a building, but Jesus knew the temple of the Holy Spirit was His body! *(And yours now too!)* You see, just because God gave you a promise and you don't see it yet, doesn't mean it's not coming. In fact, it may be happening right in front of your eyes! The way you're expecting your miracle to come, and the way God is going to give it to you, may not look the same. Remember, it's not over yet! You may feel like you're in a "losing" season right now but the good news is, God has some special abilities that He loves to use when we're "losing." It should be incredibly encouraging to know that Jesus has already overcome the world. There is nothing that can stop you from victory in Jesus. God is working in the midst of what may feel like a losing battle for you today. The promise He gave you, whatever that may be, whatever it is you're believing for, it is on its way! Just be open to receiving it in a way that you may have never dreamed of! A *Kansas City shuffle* is when you use the old "bait and switch" on someone who is too smart for their own good. Your enemy, the devil, thinks he has you beaten. He thinks he has you down for the count. But that couldn't be further from the truth! What he may use to bring you down, God will switch it around and use the same thing to lift you up, give you victory, and put that devil right back in his place!

LET ME CHALLENGE YOU TODAY

Don't be discouraged today thinking God has forgotten about you or your dreams. He hasn't. I promise you. Jesus has NEVER failed anyone and He won't start today with you. That should be extremely comforting! He is at the right hand of the Father right now praying for you, on your behalf, and His hand is ALWAYS at work! Keep thanking Him for the miracle you're believing for until you DO see it. Because who knows, it may be right in front of you already!

LET ME PRAY FOR YOU TODAY

Thank You, Jesus, that we have victory in YOU today! Even if we don't see it or feel it God, we know we can trust Your Word. Thank You that Your timing is perfect. Forgive us if we have ever doubted You. Today please give us a fresh peace and reassurance that You are still working in & through us *and* in our situation. God, we thank You today, that what the devil meant to destroy us, You will use it to build us into overcomers who look more like You!
In Jesus' name, Amen.

What is God speaking to you today?

_____

_____

_____

_____

_____

_____

_____

_____

_____

_____

_____

_____

_____

_____

_____

_____

_____

_____

_____

_____

_____

_____

12. THATS SICK!

LUKE 19:4

"So he ran ahead and climbed a sycamore tree beside the road, for Jesus was going to pass that way."

THINK ABOUT THAT FOR A MINUTE

Are you an outdoorsy person? Is that even a word? OUTDOORSY? Well, I am NOT. Not at all! I love the great INDOORS! If there is no WIFI or AC, it's not for me! I remember as a boy, though, I grew up on a bit of a farm. *It wasn't a farm.* It was a normal house in a normal neighborhood, but no one told my mom that! We had horses, pigs, goats, chickens, you name it, all running around our backyard. This was definitely not my cup of tea. One day I was outside playing when our male goat, Arthur, who had HUGE horns, decided to chase me. He came charging at me and I was terrified! I started running for my life! I couldn't outrun him, but I was so desperate to get away from him that I finally ran straight up a tree, where I sat for what seemed like hours before my mom found me and saved me. In our verse today we see that Zacchaeus is running towards a sycamore tree to climb so that he can see Jesus. Now this doesn't sound like anything too crazy until you understand how things worked back in this time period. You see, people back then didn't just *run for fun*. Think about it, did you ever read a scripture that said, "Jesus ran quickly?" No! He walked everywhere He went. You see running was only done out of necessity or desperation, but to climb a tree, that was unheard of. So why would Zacchaeus do this? Well, if we remember from Sunday school, "*Zacchaeus was a wee little man and a wee little man was he.*" But was the only reason he climbed that tree due to his stature? I don't think so. I think it was out of desperation. Zacchaeus had a need in his life that was greater than his pride. He KNEW he needed Jesus and he was determined to see Him no matter what. I think God is so funny sometimes. Why did he climb a *SYCAMORE* tree? You see, I believe Zacchaeus was *SICK* of his life and wanted *MORE*. He was *SICK OF MORE* stress than peace. I believe he was *SICK OF MORE* curses than blessings, *SICK OF* MORE pain than joy. When we finally get to the point of desperation, the point where our need for Jesus outweighs our need for acceptance from other people around us, that's when we are able to do whatever it takes to get to Jesus!

LET ME CHALLENGE YOU TODAY

What are you sick of today? What things in your life are causing you frustration and keeping you from the promises God has for you? Get desperate today! Whatever it is you feel you need more of today, Jesus is the answer! Don't be afraid to run to Him, cry out to Him, and let Him know you NEED Him in every area of your life! He will fill you with more joy than you can handle. I promise!

LET ME PRAY FOR YOU TODAY

God, we thank You today, that You love us enough to see us right where we are. We thank You that we're not going through any of this alone. Father, we acknowledge our need and desperation for You. We bring to You all of our needs and burdens today and lay them at Your feet. We are DESPERATE for You, God! Thank You for reaching into all the empty spots in our lives today and filling us with Your peace and joy til' overflowing! In Jesus' name, Amen.

What is God speaking to you today?

_____

_____

_____

_____

_____

_____

_____

_____

_____

_____

_____

_____

_____

_____

_____

_____

_____

_____

_____

_____

_____

_____

_____

13. WHAT A RIDICULOUS QUESTION

MARK 10:50-52

Bartimaeus threw aside his coat, jumped up, and came to Jesus. "What do you want me to do for you?" Jesus asked. "My Rabbi, the blind man said, "I want to see!" And Jesus said to him, "Go, for your faith has healed you." Instantly the man could see, and he followed Jesus down the road.

THINK ABOUT THAT FOR A MINUTE

I have a beautiful little sister named Rachael. She is just a joy to be around andI love her very much. Growing up with her took us to many Special Olympics competitions for her to compete in. If you have never heard of the Special Olympics, it is the world's largest sports organization for children and adults with intellectual disabilities & physical disabilities. It is truly an amazing organization and the events are so fun to attend. That being said, I have been around handicapped/disabled children and adults almost my entire life, so when I first read today's verse, there is a line that I find extremely funny and ridiculous at the same time. You see, we find "Blind Bartimaeus" sitting beside the road crying out for Jesus to have mercy on him. Jesus hears his cry and tells Bartimaeus to come to Him. The Bible then tells us that Bartimaeus got up and "came" to Jesus. Some translations even say he "RAN" to Jesus. Here's what I find to be very humorous. Bartimaeus gets to Jesus and Jesus has the *audacity* to ask, "What do you need?" Is that not hilarious and ridiculous to you?! Listen, I've seen many races in the Special Olympics over the years and I can't say that I've ever seen a blind man run in one. But if I did, I bet there is one thing for CERTAIN I could tell you, *THAT GUY IS BLIND!* Right?! It doesn't say, "They helped Bartimaeus get to Jesus". It says He came on his own. He ran on his own. I guarantee you it was quite obvious that this man was blind, so why would Jesus ask him, "What do you need?" I mean, come on Jesus, the guy is clearly blind! HE NEEDS TO SEE! When you ignore what Jesus is AC-TUALLY trying to accomplish here, the question may seem mean. *Jesus was 100% man but He was also 100% God.* I know that He knew that Bartimaeus was blind. He also knew that He was about to heal him. So why would God ask such a crazy question? Has God ever asked you a *ridiculous* question? If He hasn't yet, just wait. He will! I think that's one of God's favorite things to do, to ask us ridiculous questions. The key here is to understand WHY. You see God knows EVERYTHING. When God asks you a question, you need to remember He's not actually looking for an answer. He already knows the answer. What He REALLY wants to know is what your REVELATION of the question He's asking is. Does that make sense? He wasn't actually asking *Blind Bartimaeus* what he needed. He was asking, "What do you BELIEVE I can do for you?" When you feel God asking you a question that is seemingly ridiculous, next time remember that He's not looking for a right or wrong answer, He just wants to see what you BELIEVE He can take care of for you. You see, the verse ends with Jesus saying, "Go, your FAITH has healed you." Meaning, it was his belief that caused the healing! Jesus paid for your salvation, your redemption, and your healing 2000 years ago on the cross. Now He just wants you to BELIEVE that.

LET ME CHALLENGE YOU TODAY

What is the revelation you have about Jesus today? Do you see Him as the *'meeter'* of ALL your needs? Or are you still trying to make things happen on your own today? Let me encourage you to RUN to Jesus today! Whatever it is, please know that He is the One who can help. He is the One who can make it happen. Let the realization sink in that He already paid it ALL for You. He just wants you to RUN to Him now!

LET ME PRAY FOR YOU TODAY

Father, we thank You today for loving us enough to even ASK us ridiculous questions. God, give us a fresh revelation today of who You are and how much You love us. I pray that You increase our capacity to understand how mighty and awesome You are today, God. Father, we choose to believe You and Your word over our own thoughts and circumstances. In Jesus' name, Amen.

What is God speaking to you today?

_____

_____

_____

_____

_____

_____

_____

_____

_____

_____

_____

_____

14. THE JOY OF THE LORD

Nehemiah 8:10b

""Do not grieve, for the joy of the LORD is your strength."

THINK ABOUT THAT FOR A MINUTE

In Nehemiah 8, the people of Israel have returned from exile in Babylon, and Ezra the priest is reading the *Law of Moses* to them. As they hear the words of the law, they are convicted of their sins and begin to weep. Nehemiah tells them not to grieve, but to celebrate instead, because the *joy of the Lord* is their strength. Let's look at 3 questions about the Joy of the Lord. First, *what is the joy of the Lord?* The joy of the Lord is not merely happiness or pleasure, but a deep-seated sense of well-being that comes from knowing and trusting in God. It is a joy that transcends our circumstances and is rooted in the character of God. This joy is not dependent on external factors, but is the fruit of the Holy Spirit dwelling within us. Secondly, *how does the joy of the Lord give us strength?* When we are filled with the joy of the Lord, we are able to face the challenges of life with confidence and courage. It doesn't mean there WON'T BE challenges, we can just go through them with a joy that doesn't belong to ourselves! We know that

God is in control and that He is faithful to His promises. This gives us a sense of peace that passes understanding and enables us to persevere through difficult times. The joy of the Lord also gives us a perspective that is focused on eternity rather than the temporal. We are able to endure hardships because we know that our ultimate hope is in Christ. Lastly, *how can we cultivate the joy of the Lord?* We can cultivate the joy of the Lord in several ways. First, we must prioritize our relationship with God through prayer, reading His Word, and worship. Like we're doing now! As we spend time in His presence, we will experience the joy that comes from knowing Him. Secondly, we can cultivate joy by choosing to be grateful for what God has done for us. When we focus on His blessings rather than our struggles, our perspective shifts, and we are able to find joy in the midst of difficulty. Finally, we can cultivate joy by serving others. When we give of ourselves to help others, we experience the joy of making a difference in someone's life. Remember this when going through the mess of life. The joy of the Lord is our strength. When we cultivate this joy through our relationship with God, gratitude, and service, then we are able to face the challenges of life with confidence and courage. As we trust in God's faithfulness and focus on eternity, we find a deep-seated sense of well-being that transcends our circumstances. One of the greatest truths on this planet is that the joy of the Lord is our strength!

LET ME CHALLENGE YOU TODAY

Today let your focus be on how the joy of the Lord is such a powerful force! It can give us the strength to face the challenges of life. By seeking joy in God through worship, gratitude, service, and fellowship we can experience the joy of the Lord and find the strength we need to live the life God has called us to live. A JOYFUL life!

LET ME PRAY FOR YOU TODAY

God, thank You that YOUR joy is OUR strength! Today, Father, we make a choice to cast our cares on You. Regardless of the situation or season of life we find ourselves in today, we choose to make Your joy our strength. Thank You for a fresh peace and love today as we move forward in the strength of Your joy! In Jesus' name, Amen.

What is God speaking to you today?

_____

_____

_____

_____

_____

_____

_____

_____

_____

_____

_____

_____

_____

_____

_____

_____

_____

_____

_____

_____

_____

15. LOVE - LOVE

COLOSSIANS 4:6

Let your conversation be gracious and attractive. so that you will have the right response for everyone.

THINK ABOUT THAT FOR A MINUTE

In 1998 it was my sophomore year of high school and I was a bit of a class clown that often got into trouble for talking too much. After a brief meeting with the principal one afternoon, it was suggested to me that I use my "skills" for something productive rather than disturbing to the class. Thus began my high school career in speech and debate. I have never even HEARD of speech and debate till that moment. I won 1st place in every single speech and debate tournament that I entered that year. I love to debate! I love the idea of a battle with words. I even got into some rap battles in my early twenties *but we won't talk about that.* The problem with debate though, is that it's not a healthy form of communication. Don't get me wrong, it's fun, and there is a time and place for it. But doesn't it seem to you like almost every encounter we have with strangers, friends or even family feels like a debate? Or better yet, it can *feel like a battle* at times. What if we have been communicating wrong our entire lives? Our scripture today tells us that every word we speak should be gracious, loving, and kind. We should be encouraging everyone we speak to, every time we speak to them. The problem is, most people see communicating as a tennis match when they should see it as a game of catch. Let me explain. In tennis the object is to hit the ball and get the other person to miss it. You're trying to score a point. You're trying to win. In catch, however, the object of the game is to get the ball into the other player's glove so that they can, in return, get it back to yours. In other words, communication shouldn't be a competition, rather it should be an opportunity to love like Jesus with every word we speak. There will be so many people who never set foot in a church. The only encounter they may have with Jesus is when they encounter you. This is only one scripture out of hundreds I could have chosen for this topic, so it's very clear to me that God wants us to be very intentional about every word we speak. This is so that we can build people up and ultimately lead them to Jesus. I find it ironic that a score of 0-0 in tennis is called love-love. Because when both people truly understand that the score for every conversation and encounter should always be 0-0, that's when we have entered into love-love and it's all because of His love!

LET ME CHALLENGE YOU TODAY

Be INTENTIONAL with your words today. Go into every conversation and every encounter prepared to play a game of catch, not having a tennis match. Remember that your words carry power. God created the world using His words, and you are creating your world around you using your words. Let every word you say today be full of grace, ready to build up and encourage as many people as you can. You never know who God is placing on your path just so you can bless them today. This world can be a dark place but you carry the light of Christ inside of you. Let it out with every word you speak!

LET ME PRAY FOR YOU TODAY

Father, I thank You for Your love! Thank You for giving us the perfect example of how to communicate with others through Your Son Jesus. Today help us keep in mind, "What would Jesus do?" in every conversation we have. Let us use our words to spread Your love to everyone we encounter today. Thank You for reminding us how important our words really are. May we use them to give You all honor and glory today! In Jesus' name, Amen.

What is God speaking to you today?

_____

_____

_____

_____

_____

_____

_____

_____

_____

_____

_____

_____

_____

_____

_____

_____

_____

_____

_____

16. MY DAD CAN BEAT UP YOUR DAD

EXODUS 14:14

The Lord himself will fight for you. Just stay calm.

THINK ABOUT THAT FOR A MINUTE

Do you remember when you were a child growing up? Eventually during recess at school or playing with friends you would have some sort of altercation. Words would start to heat up, the idea of *"telling"* or getting a parent to come out may be brought up? But then somewhere down the line it would turn into, "my dad can beat up your dad!" Do you recall hearing that? Or maybe it was you who said that? I don't know why kids say that, it's not like our dads were ACTUALLY going to come outside and square up with each other to settle the argument of 7 year-olds. Even as I'm typing this, it does sound like something I would do *(I'm kidding... I think).* There was just always something so reassuring about knowing I could go get my dad! To a child, a dad can do ANYTHING. But there comes a time when that seems to change. As we get older we start to feel more independent and want to do things for our-selves. I think this describes us spiritually as well. When we first come to Jesus it's such a joy and relief trusting God with everything. We pray about every little issue and problem, we thank Him for each day, each breath, and even each close parking space by the door! It's so new and freeing. But down the line somewhere we stop taking "everything" to God. We get comfortable in our relationship with God and we start trying to do things in our own strength and in our own way. We think becoming "spiritually mature" means we can handle more, but what it should mean is that we lean on Jesus even more! *I love that the Bible tells us to come to Him like a little child.* We need that mentality. When trouble comes into our lives, when the storms of life show up out of nowhere, we need to remember, "My dad can beat up your dad!" I'm being funny, but I'm also 100% serious. We need to *remember who our Father is.* Not only remember who He is, but also remember, *He has NEVER lost a fight!* He NEVER will. This is key to remember, because when you decide to try and resolve your problems on your own, essentially what you're telling God is, "I don't need You in this fight, Father! I can handle it on my own." When we say this, even metaphorically, to God, He allows us to fight on our own. He's such a *good* Father, He would never stand in our way. However, if you will LET Him, just like our scripture today tells us, *He will fight for you!* You can just stay calm and rest assured KNOWING your Father is fighting for you, and He has NEVER lost a fight.

LET ME CHALLENGE YOU TODAY

Whatever it is that has been heavy on your mind, and weighing you down, just tell it today, "*My dad can beat up your dad!*" This is just a fun and easy way to remind yourself that you have a good, good Father who loves you more than anything and that wants to fight this battle for you! And the best part is, He has NEVER lost a fight, so you know you can't lose! You get to rest while God takes care of the mess. Be intentional today to truly cast all your cares on Christ, because He really does care for you.

LET ME PRAY FOR YOU TODAY

God, we thank You today that You are willing to fight every battle we may encounter for us. We ask that You help us to remember that we can rest in You today, while You fight our battles for us. Renew our minds today Father, to that of a child, with the perfect belief that my "Dad" can take care of anything! We are so grateful that You have never lost a battle and You won't start losing today. Thank You for a total peace that goes beyond our understanding as we trust You with every situation and battle in our lives. In Jesus' name, Amen.

What is God speaking to you today?

17. THANK YOU

Psalms 100:4

Enter his gates with thanksgiving; go into his courts with praise. Give thanks to him and praise his name.

THINK ABOUT THAT FOR A MINUTE

Have you noticed yet how many times we say "thank you" in this book during our prayer? Did you know that is intentional? I think the question I get asked the most while I'm out preaching is, "How do I get into the presence of God?" I also hear, "How do I hear God's voice?" I understand that these can be very frustrating issues in your walk with God as a new believer, or even someone who has grown up in Christianity their whole life. It's frustrating when you KNOW you NEED His presence, but you can't seem to find it! It's like when I lock the keys in my car. The thing I need is right in front of me! I know WHAT I need, I can even see it, but I just can't access it! If you feel that way, or ever have, let me help you out today! There IS a magic phrase to get into the presence of God! It's not ABRACADABA, it's *THANK YOU!* Our scripture today tells us that we enter His gates with THANKSGIVING and we en-

68

ter His courts with praise! We forget sometimes that the Bible doesn't always make things difficult. In fact, this is as clear as it gets! But the devil is such a good liar. We feel like we have to BEG God for what we need. But the truth is, He already paid for ALL your needs 2000 years ago on the cross! He paid for your salvation, yes, but also your healing and deliverance. We don't have to beg God for anything! *We just need to THANK Him for what He's already done*! I heard someone say once, "Kelly, I don't know what to thank Him for." That's a very honest statement. If you feel that way, start by thanking Him for what He DIDN'T do. You heard me right. Thank Him for the guy/girl you THOUGHT you wanted to marry, but now you're so glad you didn't! Thank Him for the job you thought you wanted, etc. If you start thanking Him for what He DIDN'T do, it won't take you long at all to start seeing what He HAS done for you! Gratitude and thanksgiving will open more doors than you can ever imagine. If you will remember that every time you thank God that you are entering into His presence, I guarantee you'll start LOOKING for reasons to thank Him! It won't won't be long before you're thanking Him all day long. These will be the best days of your life, because you will be in His presence ALL DAY. Try it today and watch what happens!

LET ME CHALLENGE YOU TODAY

Let's change the way we pray and talk to God today. Let's stop begging Him for what He already paid the price for. Let's start THANKING our way into His presence. As you begin to make "thank you" your new favorite words, take an inventory of where your life is, because those 2 words are about to change EVERY-THING for you. It'll be fun to look back and see just how powerful time in His presence has been.

LET ME PRAY FOR YOU TODAY

Lord Jesus, THANK YOU, THANK YOU, THANK YOU! We are so grateful for all that was given for us. Thank You, that You paid it ALL on the cross for us! Thank You today for the revelation that we don't have to beg You for anything! You are a good, good Father who loves His children. We thank You for making clear the "secret" words that lead us into Your presence. Help us today to remember to use these words often. *Thank You!* In Jesus' name, Amen.

What is God speaking to you today?

_____

_____

_____

_____

_____

_____

_____

_____

_____

_____

_____

_____

_____

_____

_____

_____

_____

_____

_____

18. STICK TO THE PLAN

MARK 6:48

He saw that they were in serious trouble, rowing hard and struggling against the wind and waves. About three o'clock in the morning Jesus came toward them, walking on the water. He intended to go past them.

THINK ABOUT THAT FOR A MINUTE

Don't you just hate it when you have an event or activity all planned out and then something unexpected comes along and ruins everything? I don't think there is anything more annoying than spontaneous delays. I remember watching the Super Bowl in 2013 when a huge thunderstorm hit. In the middle of the game they had to stop playing and enter a 2 hour long "rain delay" because of all the lightning in the area. It felt like the whole country was annoyed all at the same time! I can only imagine this is only a fraction of how the disciples felt in today's scripture. Jesus told them to get in the boat and head across the water. He was going to go pray and told them that He would meet up with them on the other side. Now this plan sounds all well and fine but I don't think the disciples planned on running into the most massive storm they had ever seen! Pay attention to what this scripture says! Jesus sees that they are in trouble and fighting for their lives. He starts coming towards them, walking on the water! Is He going to stop and help? NOPE! It says, "He intended to go past them!" What?! This is crazy! Why wouldn't Jesus stop to help? You see, we can relate to this story so very well can't we? We find ourselves in storms all the time. We cry out to God for help. But so many times it FEELS like God doesn't hear us. It FEELS like Jesus is just walking past us in the middle of our struggle. I asked God, "Why wasn't Jesus going to stop and help them?" And here is what I felt God was saying to me, *"The plan never changed. I told them to meet me on the other side"* That was the plan. The wind, the waves, the storm... none of those things changed the plan. They just stole your focus! You see, whatever God has spoken into your life, whatever the plan is you know He has called you to, doesn't change when things get hard. *His promise still stands.* I know life seems to get in the way. We find ourselves in storms all the time. He never promised us an easy ride. But He did promise to always be there with us in the middle of the storm! The good news is, even though Jesus INTENDED to walk past them, He didn't. He stopped and helped them. And that's what He will do for you too. The plan for your life hasn't changed. Keep your faith strong knowing He sees you in the middle of your struggle, but He will NEVER let you sink! Just stay in the story.

LET ME CHALLENGE YOU TODAY

I don't know if you're in a "storm" today or not. But I know that if you aren't, it's only a matter of time until you are. God tells us in this life we will have many trials and troubles. The good news is, He will be right there with you! So take heart today. Remember that the plan has never changed! Whatever God has told you He has for you, His promise is good! No storm can ever take away or change His plan for your life! So let's stick to the plan and stay in the story!

LET ME PRAY FOR YOU TODAY

Father, we thank You today that we never have to go through the storms of life on our own. We thank You that no matter how rough things seem to be all around us, Your plan hasn't changed! Thank You that You are a good, good Father and You have great things planned for each of us. Give us the courage, faith, and focus to keep our eyes on YOU no matter what things look like around us. You are faithful and for that we give You praise! In Jesus' name, Amen.

What is God speaking to you today?

_____

_____

_____

_____

_____

_____

_____

_____

_____

_____

_____

_____

_____

_____

_____

_____

_____

_____

_____

_____

19. WHALE OF A TALE

JONAH 1:12

"Throw me into the sea," Jonah said, "and it will become calm again. I know that this terrible storm is all my fault."

THINK ABOUT THAT FOR A MINUTE

Our verse today comes from the story of Jonah and the whale. Obviously, sometimes we can know a story so well that we think, *"there isn't possibly anything NEW I can learn from this!"* But I want to challenge you to look at the story of Jonah a little differently today. When we think of this story we generally focus on Jonah or the whale. I mean, they ARE the main characters after all. However, let's shift our focus today. Jonah was a prophet and God told him to go preach a message of repentance to Ninaveah. But Jonah didn't like the sound of God's plan, so he decided to get on a boat and head in the opposite direction. Jonah is ATTEMPTING to run from God. It's a pretty bold move on Jonah's part to think he can actually run away from someone who is literally EVERY-WHERE! Jonah may not have been the brightest prophet in the box. So he gets on this boat and he is TRYING to run from God. But God sends a massive storm to show up! It's such a brutal storm that everyone on the boat is afraid for their lives. And the scripture says that *Jonah KNEW it was his fault!* He must have realized at some point, this storm isn't going to stop anytime soon, this must be God, and I better own up. So he did. He told the captain and the crew that the storm was his fault and that if they threw him overboard that the winds and waves would stop. Now here is where I want us to shift our focus today. Have you ever wondered how many OTHER people were on that boat? 30? 40? 50? Who knows exactly, but I bet it was a lot. Have you ever been through a "storm" in your life but you couldn't understand why? You're going to church. You're tithing. You're doing everything right as far as you know, but your life still seems to be in a storm? Look at this story, everyone on that boat was going through a life threatening storm, but it had NOTHING to do with them and everything to do with WHO THEY LET ON THEIR BOAT! Your life could be going through storms that you don't have to go through and it may have nothing to do with you and everything to do with the people you're spending your time with. Don't get me wrong, the Bible tells us to love everyone. But we need to be very intentional about who we allow to go through the most intimate and personal parts of our lives with us. *As iron sharpens iron, so a friend sharpens a friend.* The people around you are either pushing you closer to God or pulling you further from Him. There is NO middle ground.

LET ME CHALLENGE YOU TODAY

Examine the relationships you have in your life today. Are your closest and most intimate relationships helping you grow in your walk with God? Or are they causing you to suffer through unnecessary storms? Be intentional about who you CHOOSE to spend your time with today. And just as you want good, godly, encouraging friends around you, remember to BE a good, godly, encouraging friend to those around you as well!

LET ME PRAY FOR YOU TODAY

Father, we thank You so much for the fresh revelation of Your Word today. God, we ask that You show us any areas in our relationships that we may need to work on today. We give You access to search our hearts, examine our motives for each of our friendships, and we give You full authority to speak to us about what You want us to do. God please mold us and develop us into good, godly, encouraging friends today. And thank You for sending new friends into our lives that will help build us up and look more like You! In Jesus' name, Amen.

What is God speaking to you today?

_____

_____

_____

_____

_____

_____

_____

_____

_____

_____

_____

_____

_____

_____

_____

_____

_____

_____

_____

_____

_____

20. JESUS IS MY BFF

John 15:12-14

This is my commandment that you love another just as I have loved you.

Greater love has no one than this, that one lay down his life for his

friends. You are my friends if you do what I command.

THINK ABOUT THAT FOR A MINUTE

Friendships are such an amazing and important part of our daily lives. There is nothing better than receiving an uplifting compliment from a friend. Or even a never-ending thread of memes back and forth in your texts can brighten the day. Friends just make our days better! And it doesn't take long for you to figure out that good friends don't just come along everyday, and when you find a GREAT friend, or even a BFF, you know the value of finding such an amazing treasure. How incredible is it that the *Creator of the Universe* not only LOVES you, but WANTS to be FRIENDS with you too! That should just completely bless your day! Jesus gave everything so that we could have a friendship with Him. He literally says in our scripture today, *"this is the greatest love possible."* But pay attention, it's the last verse that changes everything! "You are My friends IF YOU DO WHAT I COMMAND." His command? "To lay down your life for your friend."I hear people say all the time that they WANT to be friends with Jesus, but my question to you is, are you truly willing to DIE to yourself every single day to get that friendship? Because what Jesus told us in our verse today is, "that's what I did for you." Wow. Let that sink in. Jesus wanted a friendship with YOU so badly, that He gave His life for it.That's a powerful love my friends. Listen, it's time to stop carrying around the things of your past, truly set aside anything in your life that is not pleasing to God, and give EVERYTHING to Him. I can promise you it will be worth it, because we already learned, there is NO GREATER love than to lay YOUR life down for a friend! And Jesus is most definitely a friend worth dying for! (*And He thinks the same about you! *wink*)

LET ME CHALLENGE YOU TODAY

Today take some time and get quiet before the Lord. Let it sink in just how special you are to God. He wanted a friendship with you so much that He gave His own life to make it happen. Now look at the friendship you've given back to God. Did you give your life for Him too? Not just bits and pieces, but ALL of it? Take a long hard look and if you see an area of your life that you realize you haven't given up yet, today is the day! Nothing is greater than laying down your life for a friend! Jesus is the ONLY friend who will give you back so much more than you give up!

LET ME PRAY FOR YOU TODAY

God, we thank You today for the gift of Your friendship. Thank You that You care enough about each and everyone of us to offer full and total access to Your friendship. God please show us any areas that we may be holding onto in our lives that we need to give up to You. Father, we make the choice today to die to ourselves. We don't want to be friends with this world any longer, we want to be friends with You! In Jesus' name, Amen.

What is God speaking to you today?

_____

_____

_____

_____

_____

_____

_____

_____

_____

_____

_____

_____

_____

_____

_____

_____

_____

_____

_____

_____

_____

_____

_____

21. JESUS TAKE THE WILL

Colossians 3:17

And whatever you do or say, do it as a representative of the Lord Jesus,
giving thanks through Him to God the Father.

THINK ABOUT THAT FOR A MINUTE

I think the one question most Christians have in common is, "
What is the will of God for my life? WHAT DOES GOD WANT ME
TO DO?!" If this is you, don't get frustrated! I will try to help give
you some guidance today! In our scripture here, it says, "In
WHATEVER you do... Do it for Jesus." What does that mean? I'm
so glad you asked. This means the importance of the will of God
for your life is more about HOW you do, than WHAT you do. Does
that make sense? Satan would love to have your mind all caught
up in trying to "figure out" the will of God for your life so that you
miss the fact that God actually wants to use you right where you
are RIGHT NOW! Doing exactly what you're already doing, but
doing it to the best of your ability, as if you were doing it directly for
Jesus! Listen, this should set you free today. Stop spending so

much time worrying about "what" to do for God. Go and do what you're already doing with EXCELLENCE, because you're doing it for JESUS! Our ultimate mission is to let people see and experience the love of Jesus through us. God knows where you are right now. He sees you. Maybe this isn't your dream job but God still has a plan to use you right where you are! When you do EVERY job or task as if you're doing it for the Lord, it may look way different than everyone else around you.

Most people simply do the bare minimum just to get by. But when you tackle every task for JESUS, people will start to notice. And it won't take long before people start to ask, "why do you do so much more than everyone else?" Why do you go above and beyond?" Then you will get to explain the love and joy of Christ they are seeing in YOUR life! It's truly amazing how something as simple as changing our mindset about WHY and HOW we do our job can actually help us and others grow closer to Jesus! Today, be thankful and grateful for where you are! Know that you are on a mission for Jesus! Ultimately, no matter what our "title" is, our JOB is to tell as MANY people as we can about the love of Jesus! And the best way to do that is to let people SEE Jesus in your life! When you change your mind about HOW you do your "job" it won't matter what or where you work, because Jesus is always the boss wherever you go! And it feels SO GOOD to hear Him say, "Well done my good and faithful servant!" at the end of every day!

LET ME CHALLENGE YOU TODAY

Stop focusing so much on "WHAT am I supposed to do?", and shift your focus to "HOW" you do what you're already doing! We serve a God of order and once He sees us stewarding well in what He has given us, that's when He tends to promote us! If you love where you are, or hate where you are, all it takes is a simple change of mind to find yourself right in the middle of His purpose for your life, and THAT is a wonderful place to be!

LET ME PRAY FOR YOU TODAY

Father, thank You for Your perfect plan for our lives. God no matter where we may be in this moment right now, we are so grateful that You have a plan for us. Thank You that You want to use us right now, today, right where we are! God, we dedicate every task to You today. No matter how big or small, God, we want to honor You in ALL we do. Thank You for the opportunity to shine Your light today on everyone we come in contact with. God we want to see YOUR Kingdom come and YOUR will be done, on Earth as it is in Heaven. In Jesus' name, Amen.

What is God speaking to you today?

_____

_____

_____

_____

_____

_____

_____

_____

_____

_____

_____

_____

_____

_____

_____

_____

_____

_____

_____

_____

_____

22. SUPERHERO CHECK LIST

John 14:12

I tell you the truth, anyone who believes in me will do the same works I have done, and even greater works, because I am going to be with the Father.

THINK ABOUT THAT FOR A MINUTE

This may be my absolute favorite scripture of all time. Did you read what that verse said? This is Jesus speaking, saying we can do the same things He did and even greater! That should blow your mind! But let me ask you a couple questions. Did you know the Bible says that we can do the same things Jesus did and even greater? You did? Ok, now let me ask, are you doing the same things Jesus did and even greater? Ahh . . . . You see, that's the problem. What Jesus is saying here is, now that He's with the Father, you and I get the same Holy Spirit He has. So WE have the power to do the same things He did! WOW! We can lay our hands on the sick and they will recover. We can speak to evil spirits and they have to flee. This should be really exciting news! I don't know if you have noticed or not but our entire world is obsessed with superheroes. I mean, Marvel, not DC, obviously (haha), but everywhere you look, it's Iron Man, Spider Man, Thor! I get it, we love superheroes. But think about this, our scripture today pretty much says, YOU are a superhero. Did you catch that? We live in a hurting, lost, dying world. But there's power inside of you that can change everything! You're a superhero! I know what you're probably thinking, "No, that's a stretch today, Kelly. I'm not a superhero." Ok, fair enough. But can I prove it to you? Every superhero has 3 things in common. Use it as a checklist, if you will, to see if you're a superhero. 1.) All superheroes have an emotional backstory that led or pushed them to become a superhero. Look, nobody ever got saved because their life was so great and everything was so perfect that they just decided, " I need to give my life to Jesus today!" That has never happened. You gave your life to Jesus because you had an emotional moment where you realized that you were never going to be good enough and you needed a savior. Every person's salvation story is an emotional backstory that led them to the superpower that now lives inside of them. 2.) All superheroes have a super villain. Darkness makes us realize the importance of light. If you've asked Jesus into your life, you are well aware you have a super villain. The devil prowls around seeking out people that he may devour. The good news is, I've read the end of the Bible. We win! Yes, you have a super villain, but he's already been defeated, and he knows that. The question is, do you? Anytime you see great power, you're going to see an enemy rise up. But Jesus has already defeated your enemy. That is good news! 3.) All superheroes live by the same code. We can thank Uncle Ben, but they ALL live by it. "With great power comes great responsibility." This one right here though, is where a lot of Christians drop the ball. Are you being responsible with the power Jesus died to give you? Are you looking for opportunities every single day to pray for people and see Jesus work in your life and in their life? You've been given great power and that comes with great responsibility. Don't just sit on the power that Jesus died to give you. Go out and use it. Jesus never intended His ministry to stop when He went to heaven. He intended it to go on through you!

LET ME CHALLENGE YOU TODAY

Today make the decision to be responsible with the power you've been given. The Bible always says that Jesus was moved by compassion when He saw sick, lost, or hurting people. We should be moved by compassion too. Today, when you feel the Holy Spirit urging you to pray for someone, hug someone, buy a meal for someone, or call someone, DO IT! Use what God has given you! Give this wonderful gift as freely as you have received it!

LET ME PRAY FOR YOU TODAY

Jesus, thank You for giving us the same Holy Spirit You had! We are honored to carry Your power inside of us. Today, put someone in our lives, or on our path. Move us with compassion to go ask what we can do to be a blessing. God we can't heal them, but YOU can! We may not know what to say to them, but YOU do! Thank You for using us today! We will be responsible with the power You have given us! In Jesus' name, Amen.

What is God speaking to you today?

_____

_____

_____

_____

_____

_____

_____

_____

_____

_____

_____

23. LITTLE FAITH?

Matthew 14:31

Jesus immediately reached out and grabbed him. "You have so little faith," Jesus said. "Why did you doubt me?"

THINK ABOUT THAT FOR A MINUTE

Have you ever been reading the Bible and come across a scripture that just BOTHERED you? Like no matter how long you spent meditating on it, you just couldn't figure it out? This is the one for me! Does this scripture bother you? It used to drive me crazy. We know this is the story of Peter walking on water. Pastors LOVE preaching this message! I can hear it now (in my best Southern Baptist Preacher" voice) *"Just'a keep'a your eyes'a on JESUS!"* All jokes aside, there really is so much we can learn from this story. But let me show you what rubbed me the wrong way. When Peter saw the wind and waves, he started to sink. Jesus lifted him up and said, "You have such little faith." Now time out. First, this is one of Jesus' closest friends.He's seen Jesus do so many miracles that he SHOULD have HUGE faith. I mean, come on, am I right? *AND by the way, Jesus, there were 11 other dudes who never even got out of the boat!* How could He say that Peter only had a little faith? Only 2 people have EVER walked on water, literally, Jesus and Peter. That's huge faith if there ever was huge faith. This bothered me but I know the Author of the book, so I asked God, "Why would You tell Peter that he had little faith?" God replied, " Google it." (God says the craziest things to me sometimes) So I googled the definition of 'a little' and I found 2 examples. The first definition was something small in size or stature. Which is exactly what I "thought" Jesus was saying. But the second definition blew my mind. It defines 'a little' as something short in length or duration. LIGHT BULB! You see, Jesus wasn't telling Peter that his faith was small rather He was saying it didn't last very long! No matter how big or small your faith may feel, remember it's about how long it lasts! Faith the size of a mustard seed will move a mountain, and I know you've got more faith than that! But even if you feel like you don't, be patient and trust in what God is doing in your life. He works all things for good for those who love Him and have been called according to His purpose. His timing is ALWAYS perfect, you just make sure you build a faith that lasts!

LET ME CHALLENGE YOU TODAY

Today, evaluate your faith. Think about this last week, last month, or even last year. Were you believing in God for something, but now you're not? What happened? Pick your faith back up today. It's okay if it's not HUGE faith. Remember, it's not the size that matters, it's how long it LASTS! Trust that God is always faithful with His promises! He has NEVER failed anyone! He won't start today with you!

LET ME PRAY FOR YOU TODAY

Father, thank You so much for a fresh revelation today of what it means to have LASTING faith. God, today, if we have let go of believing ANY promise You may have given to us, we make a choice to pick it back up and put our faith back in You! We trust Your timing Father. Thank You that You will NEVER leave us or forsake us. Thank You for reminding me of Your never-ending goodness! We put our faith in You and this time it's faith that lasts! In Jesus' name, Amen

What is God speaking to you today?

24. WILL YOU MARRY ME?

James 4:4-6

You're cheating on God. If all you want is your own way, flirting with the world every chance you get, you end up enemies of God and his way. And do you suppose God doesn't care? The proverb has it that "he's a fiercely jealous lover." And what he gives in love is far better than anything else you'll find.

THINK ABOUT THAT FOR A MINUTE

Now don't get discouraged already, I know today's scripture doesn't SOUND like an uplifting verse at first glance, but I promise you this may become one of your all time favorite scriptures if you just give me a minute to explain. I used the *Message Translation* for our verse today. I normally use the *NLT*, but I love the way the *Message* words the first sentence. *"YOU'RE CHEATING ON GOD, if all you want is your own way."* Wow. That's a bold statement. The *NLT* says "you adulterers." Let's break this down a bit. I don't know if you are married or not, but even if you're not, I'm sure you've been "in love" or at LEAST have had feelings of love for another person. Think about it like this, how INSANE would it be if when I proposed to my wife, she answered 'yes', but then asked if it would be okay if her old high school boyfriend moved in with us as well? WHAT!!! Are you kidding me? NO WAY!! That's completely ridiculous, right!? But then she tells me that she loves me the most but she just really enjoys having him in her life and doesn't want to give up such a great relationship. Does that make it any better? Absolutely NOT! I can't think of one person I know who would be okay with that kind of arrangement with their significant other. But you see, you and I do this to Jesus all the time. Our verse today says we are CHEATING on God if all we want is our old ways! It proceeds to say, "He is a fiercely jealous lover!" Please understand this, when Jesus gave His life on the cross for you, what He was really doing was asking you, "Will you marry Me?" He made a commitment on the cross to give literally EVERYTHING for you! He made a way for us to enter into a committed relationship *(covenant actually)* with Him! But then what do we do? We say, "YES! I want to be in a relationship with You, Jesus!" But then we try to bring all of our old boyfriends and girlfriends along too! "Jesus, I love YOU more than anything, but I'm going to keep this pornography addiction as well because I still need that in my life." We say, "Jesus YOU are my EVERYTHING, but I'm going to hold on to this bitterness and unforgiveness because I use it as protection and a reminder to not let people treat me this way again!"Is this starting to click? When you start to see your relationship with Jesus as a marriage, not just a casual relationship, you will begin to see HUGE changes in your life! And I love how this verse ends. It is a promise that what you find in HIS love is FAR GREATER than anything you can find in the world! That, my friends, is good news!

LET ME CHALLENGE YOU TODAY

Today, take a long look at your relationship with Jesus. Are you as committed to Him as He is to you? Examine yourself and see if you have brought any old "Boyfriends" or "Girlfriends" into your relationship with God. Let God know that today you have made a commitment to Him. You won't be disappointed! His love is far greater than anything you may be letting go of!

LET ME PRAY FOR YOU TODAY

Jesus, thank You for giving everything for us! We are so honored that You WANT to be in a covenant relationship with us. Today we repent of any "old relationships" we have brought into our relationship with You. We give it all to You today. You alone are worthy of our love, adoration, and praise! Thank You for loving us so perfectly! In Jesus' name, Amen.

What is God speaking to you today?

_____

_____

_____

_____

_____

_____

_____

_____

_____

_____

_____

_____

_____

_____

_____

_____

_____

_____

_____

_____

25. THE "SANTA CLAUS" SCRIPTURE

Psalms 37:4

Take delight in the Lord, and he will give you your heart's desires.

THINK ABOUT THAT FOR A MINUTE

On my right forearm I have a tattoo that says, "This Too Shall Pass." It's actually one of my favorite tattoos and I get compliments on it all the time. The funniest comment I've ever received, one that I've actually heard many times over the last 20 years, is "That's my favorite scripture!" This always makes me laugh so hard! You want to know why? Because it's NOT in the Bible at all! While this is funny, it's kind of sad, too. We live in such a biblically illiterate generation that it's actually dangerous. People just make up "wise" phrases and others assume it's God's word. That's why it's important to get into His word daily so you'll know exactly what God says! (Like you are now: good for you!) Another HUGE problem is knowing a scripture, but using it to FIT INTO your understanding, instead of letting the Bible SHAPE your understanding.

Today's verse is a key example. I've heard this verse taught so many times like it's a "Santa Claus" scripture. God is going to just give me all I want! Woohoo! I wish it worked that way. That would be amazing! While this scripture is amazing, we just need to get a grip on what it actually means. You see, it says "Take delight in the Lord and He will give you your heart's desires". This doesn't mean He is a genie ready to grant wishes. What it means is that whenever you want, above all else, to be as close to God as you possibly can, that God will start to put HIS desires in YOUR heart! Meaning, you will start to desire the same things God desires! You will want peace in all situations. You will choose faith over fear. You will want to love instead of hate. You will want to give more than you receive. You will want to be a blessing everywhere you go! Is this making sense? What's so cool about this is, when you start to desire the things God desires, HE GIVES THEM TO YOU! God has all the provisions you will ever need and when you learn that ALL you need is to be close to Him, that changes everything. When you finally get to the place where you and God desire the same things, well then I guess this DOES kind of turn into a "Santa Claus" Scripture! Because not only will He put the desires IN your heart, He will GIVE you your heart's desires when they're also HIS desires! How awesome is that?!

LET ME CHALLENGE YOU TODAY

Let's take a minute to really evaluate our desires today. What is it you want above all else? Are you feeling frustrated because it seems like you keep asking God for things and it doesn't happen? Today let God know you are laying down all your wants and desires at the foot of the cross. Let God put HIS desires in your heart! Watch the joy and peace that starts to consume you as you and God start to want the same things!

LET ME PRAY FOR YOU TODAY

God, we thank You so much for being such a good Father. Today we are giving You access to our entire hearts! Remove any desires that we may have that don't line up with what YOU desire. God, make our hearts match Yours. Give us a love for people like You. Give us hunger and passion for Your Word. Let us want what You want today Lord. And we thank You that as we start to desire what You desire, we will be so overcome with fulfillment and peace, so that we can trust and know we are right in the middle of Your presence and will for our lives. In Jesus' name, Amen.

What is God speaking to you today?

26. FIRE IT UP

Malachi 3:2-3

"But who will be able to endure it when he comes? Who will be able to stand and face him when he appears? For he will be like a blazing fire that refines metal, or like a strong soap that bleaches clothes. He will sit like a refiner of silver, burning away the dross. He will purify the Levites, refining them like gold and silver, so that they may once again offer acceptable sacrifices to the Lord."

THINK ABOUT THAT FOR A MINUTE

I think that whenever I was a kid that over half of the spankings that I received weren't because of lying, stealing, or fighting, rather they were due to playing with fire! I loved fire as a kid and still do as an adult! It just fascinates me! If you've read my book, *"Get Lit, Stay Lit, Spread It"*, then you know that when I was just 10 years old, I set a dumpster on fire and ALMOST burned down an entire apartment complex! So naturally, as a pastor now, I'm obsessed with fire in the Bible! And there is SO MUCH of it! I love that God is described as an "all consuming fire." I love that we get to compare our relationship with Jesus as "being on fire." But today I want to focus on the purification aspect of fire. The concept of purification by fire is found all throughout the Bible. You see, the process of refining metals involves heating them until the impurities rise to the surface and are burned away, leaving only the pure metal behind. In the same way, God uses trials, problems, people, and challenges in our lives to purify us and refine our faith. In our verse today, the prophet Malachi is speaking of the coming of the Lord and the refining work that He will do. The image of a refiner's fire is used to describe the process of purification, which involves heating the metal until the impurities are burned away. This imagery speaks to the intensity of the trials that we may face in our lives, but also to the end result; a purified faith that is pleasing to the Lord! In the book of *1 Peter,* Peter speaks of the purpose of trials and challenges in our lives. He acknowledges that these trials may cause us pain, discomfort, and to be honest they may just tick us off completely! But they also serve a greater purpose; to refine our faith and prove its genuineness. The comparison of gold refined by fire reinforces the idea that the end result is something of great value. Trust me friends, faith that's been refined in FIRE is the most valuable thing you can own in this life! I love *Isaiah 48:10,* "See, I have refined you, though not as silver; I have tested you in the furnace of affliction." Isaiah speaks to the idea that trials and challenges are a NECESSARY part of our spiritual growth. He uses the, *almost harsh* words, "furnace of affliction" to explain and let us know that the intensity of the trials we may face is part of the process! But also to emphasize the purpose - to refine and purify us!

LET ME CHALLENGE YOU TODAY

Trials and challenges are not something to be feared, but rather something that can lead to a purified faith that is pleasing to the Lord. Ask yourself these questions today and let God discuss them with you! What trials or challenges have I faced in my life that have led me to deeper faith? How can I view my current struggles as an opportunity for growth and refinement? What steps can I take to trust in God's refining work and allow Him to purify my faith? Today, let's embrace the process of purification by fire and trust in God's refining work in our lives!

LET ME PRAY FOR YOU TODAY

Father, we thank You today for Your refining process in our life. Today, help us change our mindset to see that the trials and troubles we face are just You burning out the impurities You see in us. Thank You for loving us enough to never quit refining us! May we get closer to You today and use the areas and issues in our life we THOUGHT were keeping us from You, but really we see, they are making us more LIKE You! In Jesus' name, Amen.

What is God speaking to you today?

27. DON'T WORRY

Philippians 4:6

Don't worry about anything; instead, pray about everything. Tell God what you need, and thank him for all he has done.

THINK ABOUT THAT FOR A MINUTE

Right now, are you feeling stressed out? Maybe you're feeling a little depressed? Kind of like the weight of the world is on your shoulders? If so, then this is for you! One of the biggest problems in our world right now is that everybody is so stressed out. But what if you could just make it go away? Well, good news! You can! Our verse today says, "Don't worry about anything, instead, pray about everything. Tell God what you need and thank Him for all He's done." I know this sounds ridiculous. Some of you may even be thinking, "Oh, don't worry? Right, cause it's that easy…" But there are a few magic words in that scripture you might miss if you're not careful. When the apostle Paul wrote these words, he made them very plain. "Don't worry about anything." Okay Paul, but how? "Instead, pray about everything. just thank Him for all that He's done!" Let me explain something to you: stress, anxiety, depression, etc., none of it can stand in the presence of the Lord.

It has to flee! So now the only question really is, "How do I get into the presence of the Lord when I'm so stressed out?" I'm glad you asked. Psalm 100:4 says, "We enter His courts with Thanksgiving, we come into His gates with praise." If you need the presence of the Lord, it only takes 2 words to get there. THANK YOU! Philippians 4 is so basic. *Don't worry, pray and thank God.* But it's so basic because it's so powerful. When you're feeling stressed, depressed, or anxious just start thanking God that you're not! Let me show you, "God I thank You for the peace that You're giving me right now, I thank You that You are with me, and I don't have to be worried about anything. I thank You that You are removing ALL stress from my life!" Now you may be thinking, "But why would I thank Him for it when I haven't experienced it yet?" *Because that's called faith.* So many times when Jesus healed in the Bible, He said, "Go, your FAITH has healed you." Faith is just believing something has happened before it actually has. So when you start thanking God in the middle of being stressed out, His presence will come upon you, and stress, anxiety, and depression HAS to leave. He's done. Now you're exercising faith and you'll find yourself in the presence of the Lord. And THAT my friends, is the best place to be!

LET ME CHALLENGE YOU TODAY

When you start to feel the weight of the world on your shoulders today, stop. Just take even one minute to realize you are feeling stressed. But then, start thanking God! Thank Him for anything you can think of! OUT LOUD if you can! When you start doing this, you will be AMAZED at how fast peace comes over you. Seriously, try it today! God WANTS to give you His presence. He wants you to have peace. It is joy for Him when OUR joy comes from HIS strength. Today is going to be a wonderful day for you if you spend it in the presence of the Lord, I promise!

LET ME PRAY FOR YOU TODAY

Father, we thank You today! We thank You for Your promises and for giving us Your peace that goes beyond our understanding. God thank You for making it so easy to come into Your presence. We give You all of our stress, anxiety, and depression today. We gladly trade You these for Your joy, love and peace. Thank You, that You are working in and on our lives so that we can continue to be more like You every day. We love You so much today! In Jesus' name, Amen.

What is God speaking to you today?

28. MAKE YOUR BED

Psalms 139:8

If I ascend into Heaven, You are there; If I make my bed in hell,

behold, You are there.

THINK ABOUT THAT FOR A MINUTE

I have always LOVED this scripture. It shows so clearly that God
is there! Where? EVERYWHERE! You can't get away from Him!
That is extremely comforting to me. Just to KNOW that at my best,
God is there and at my WORST, God is there! Take notice that it
says, if *"I" ascend* into Heaven and if *"I" make* my bed in hell. I
think it's very important to see that we are in control of where we
are going, or where we are making our bed. I don't know about
you, but I've made my bed in some pretty sketchy places a time or
two! I mean I made choices that took me so far away from God.
We tend to get mad at God when we realize how far away from
Him we actually are sometimes. But what is encouraging to me
now, is looking back, I can see how God was always right there
with me. Even in the worst moments of my life. This verse also

reminds me of Jonah. You know, *Jonah and the whale*? Jonah was a prophet. He KNEW God's word, and he knew it WELL! In fact, while he was in the belly of the whale, when he repented he quoted the book of Psalms 23 times! This means we can know scripture, we can come to church every Sunday, we can look like the best Christian ever on the outside but still have our bed made in hell. Even the most mature believer, even a prophet like Jonah, can find themselves far from God sometimes. But take comfort knowing that even if you wake up tomorrow feeling like your bed has been made in hell, feeling like you're so far away from where you KNOW you need to be, or feeling like God is a million miles away, you can take comfort knowing He's actually right there with you! Don't beat yourself up when you find your bed made in hell either! The truth is, we have all sinned and fallen short of the glory of God! That's why Jesus gave His life to make a way for us to be with Him ALWAYS! The best news in the world is that Jesus, who knew NO sin, BECAME sin! So that we, who knew NO righteousness, could BECOME the righteousness of Jesus Christ! I really can't stress enough how this verse should be a constant comfort for you. You can truly live in the peace of knowing every single day, that no matter what you do, or where you find yourself in this life, God is ALWAYS with you!

LET ME CHALLENGE YOU TODAY

Maybe today you realize that you've been making your bed in some sketchy places. You realize that you're not as close to God as you want to be. If that's you, you should also realize that God is actually with you right now! He has NEVER abandoned you. Take some time today to thank Him for that! Thank Him for the peace of knowing that, no matter what, He is ALWAYS there!

LET ME PRAY FOR YOU TODAY

Father, thank You for never leaving us! Lord, we are so encouraged by Your word today. What a comfort it is to know You are with us in our best moments, but also in our worst moments. Thank You, that even if we feel a million miles away from You, it is only one step back to You. Guide our steps Lord, may we follow Your voice everyday, so that we may NEVER make our beds in "hell" ever again! In Jesus' name, Amen.

What is God speaking to you today?

29. SANDPAPER PEOPLE

James 1:2-4

Dear brothers and sisters, when troubles of any kind come your way, consider it an opportunity for great joy. For you know that when your faith is tested, your endurance has a chance to grow. So let it grow, for when your endurance is fully developed, you will be perfect and complete, needing nothing.

THINK ABOUT THAT FOR A MINUTE

Have you ever had a person in your life that just rubbed you the wrong way? Every time you show up and they're there you think, "Oh great. Here we go again." It's like every word they say makes you grit your teeth? Like every step they take just makes you want to take a step further away? What If I told you that God puts these people in your life for a reason? And not only do they serve a purpose, but they are actually a gift from God! I like to call them, "Sandpaper People." Let me explain... Sandpaper is a tool that is designed to smooth and refine surfaces. It's a sheet or strip of abrasive paper that has particles of sand or other hard substances glued to it. Sandpaper comes in different grades, from coarse to fine, depending on the size and density of the abrasive particles. Sandpaper is used in various applications to remove roughness, rust, or old paint and prepare surfaces for painting, staining, or polishing. Hmmm.... The Bible also speaks of a refining process that God uses to shape and transform His people. In Isaiah 48:10, God says, "I have refined you, but not as silver is refined. Rather, I have refined you in the furnace of suffering." Here is what you need to know about the "Sandpaper People" in your life. God uses rough situations and people to smooth out our character. Just as sandpaper rubs against a surface to remove roughness and imperfections, God allows us to go through difficult and trying circumstances with extremely difficult people, to expose our flaws and refine our character. When we face challenges, we have a choice to either resist and complain or to trust and learn. Pay attention to our verse today, it says, "when troubles of any kind come your way, consider it an opportunity for great joy. For you know that when your faith is tested, your endurance has a chance to grow. So let it grow, for when your endurance is fully developed, you will be perfect and complete, needing nothing." Did you catch that?! God is using "Hateful Hannah" and "Grumpy Gus" to actually develop YOU into perfection! These people are a GIFT to help make you more like Jesus! God says consider these people a

JOY! It's all about a change in your mindset. God uses different grades of "sandpaper people" to achieve different levels of refinement. Just as sandpaper comes in various grits, from coarse to fine, depending on the level of smoothing required, God uses different levels of testing and trials to refine us according to His purpose. Some "sandpaper people" may be minor irritations, while others may be major crises that shake us to the core. However, in all cases, God knows what we need, and His ultimate goal is for YOU to become more like Christ.

LET ME CHALLENGE YOU TODAY

Let's work on changing our mindset today. Take a quick mental inventory of all the "sandpaper people" you know in your life. Now start thanking God for each of them. Thank Him for placing the right people in your life to help shape you more into the image of Christ. Start seeing "sandpaper people" as a joy instead of a curse. These people really are a gift if you allow them to be.

LET ME PRAY FOR YOU TODAY

God, we thank You today for changing our mindset about the "sandpaper people" in our lives. Father, we are so grateful You love us enough to put difficult people and trials in our lives so that You can refine us into who YOU have designed us to be. God we pray blessings over all those who have made our lives more difficult because we see now, it was really YOU working in us, through them, to develop us into who You have called us to be. In Jesus' name, Amen.

What is God speaking to you today?

_____

_____

_____

_____

_____

_____

_____

_____

_____

_____

_____

30. TURN! TURN! TURN!

Ecclesiastes 3:1

For everything there is a season,

a time for every activity under heaven.

THINK ABOUT THAT FOR A MINUTE

As I was growing up one of my favorite things to do was go visit my grandparents. There was nothing better than a week of junk food at Mema's house! But before we ever got to her house, the car ride itself was an amazing time! We would sing song after song as loudly as we could! One of the songs my grandma loved to sing to me was. "Turn! Turn! Turn!", made famous by the "Byrds." I still vividly remember us almost yelling those lyrics out! *"A time of love, and a time of hate; a time of war, and a time of peace."* I had absolutely NO IDEA I was actually quoting scripture! The lyrics of that song are straight out of Ecclesiastes! Ecclesiastes 3:1-11 is a well-known passage of scripture that begins with the famous words, "For everything there is a season, a time for every activity under heaven." This scripture speaks to the cyclical nature of life, the inevitability of change, and the goodness of God over all things. I absolutely love how the first eight verses of Ecclesiastes 3 describe a series of opposites that are each appropriate in their own time and season. For example, there is "a time to be born, and a time to die", "a time to weep, and a time to laugh". This reminds us that God has planned for a time and a season for everything in life. We must learn to accept and embrace the changes that come our way. We have to remember that God is in control of all things. We must trust in His plan even when we do not understand the reasons for the seasons of life. We can take comfort in the fact that God has a purpose and a plan for our lives, and that He will work all things together for good! As we reflect today on our verse, there are several important lessons that we can apply to our lives. First, we must learn to accept and embrace the changes that come our way, recognizing that there is a time and a season for everything in life. Second, we must trust in the goodness of God, even when we do not understand the reasons for the seasons of life. Finally, we must seek to live our lives in accordance with God's purposes, recognizing that He has a plan and a purpose for each of our lives. This is such a powerful reminder of the cyclical nature of life, the inevitability of change, and the goodness of God over all things. As we seek to navigate the seasons of life, let us trust in God's plan and purpose for our lives. We can rest in the peace of knowing He has it all under control and all things will work out for good in His perfect timing and season.

LET ME CHALLENGE YOU TODAY

Take some time today to acknowledge the season you're in. Don't get depressed if you're in a winter season or a season of testing. Start thanking the Lord for where you are! Because now you understand that God uses ALL seasons in our lives to develop us and all things will work out for our good in His timing, not ours!

LET ME PRAY FOR YOU TODAY

Father, thank You for how perfectly You made the world! With each season having a specific purpose. God, help us to better understand the season we find ourselves in today. Help us to remember that we can't ALWAYS live in summer, because You need to use the winter to build us and shape us into who You've called us to be! May we take joy in understanding that we can prosper in every season of life, as long as we walk through them as close to You as possible! In Jesus' name, Amen.

What is God speaking to you today?

31. THE FALSE PROTAGONIST

GALATIANS 2:20

My old self has been crucified with Christ. It is no longer I who live, but Christ lives in me. So I live in this earthly body by trusting in the Son of God, who loved me and gave himself for me.

THINK ABOUT THAT FOR A MINUTE

I know what you're thinking, "What is a "False Protagonist?" Well, I'll explain. I absolutely love movies! And my favorite kind are movies that have a huge plot twist! The best form of twist, in my opinion, is when they use the "false protagonist." A protagonist is the main character of the story. The movie "Psycho" by Alfred Hitchcock, was the first movie to use this technique. You THINK you're watching the story of Marion Crane who stole a lot of money and is trying to leave town to meet up with her boyfriend. She finds herself in the middle of a huge storm on the way and decides to stop at a cute, quaint, little place called, "The Bates Motel." Then, 47 minutes into the movie, (*Spoiler alert - even though you've had like, 50 years to watch it)* she gets killed in the iconic shower scene. What?! They killed off the main character in the movie?! Yes! To identify the REAL protagonist of the story, Norman Bates! Everyone watching is left in shock! It really is an amazing story telling technique. But I don't think I can give Alfred Hitchcock all the credit. God has been doing this for a LONG time. Our scripture today should show you that there needs to be, no, HAS to be, a false protagonist twist in your story too! There has to come a time when you realize that this life is NOT about you! It's about Jesus! That's why we have to make a choice to die to ourselves so that it's not us in control of our lives, but rather Jesus. The truth is that Jesus is the main character in EVERY story ever told. When the people around us, who are watching our lives see us, well they should be seeing Jesus instead. And when you decide to make this change, your audience will be left in shock! To most people, it doesn't make sense to let God be first in their life. It doesn't make sense to live a life for Jesus. But it does for those who understand the false protagonist. Everyday, as a reminder, I like to say, "My story is HISTORY!" Which has a twofold meaning. One, my story doesn't matter. My past doesn't matter. My old life is gone. My mistakes are in the past. My story is history! And two, my story is HIS story. My life is not about me anymore. I live to make the name of Jesus great, not my own. Everything I do, let Jesus get the glory, and let the people watching my life see HIM and not me. THAT'S the "False Protagonist!"

LET ME CHALLENGE YOU TODAY

Take a moment to look over your life and see if you can pinpoint the moment of your "false protagonist" twist. Can you remember when you made the choice to say, "Jesus, it's" about You and not me? If not, today may be your "47 minute" mark in your movie! Let God show you how amazing your story really can be when HE is the main character! And if you have done that, take some time to reflect on how much different your life is now! Give God the praise and let Him know that this is only the beginning! We're going to keep Him in the spotlight!

LET ME PRAY FOR YOU TODAY

Jesus, thank You so much for giving Your life for us. We honor You by giving our lives back to You today. We ask You to come and be the main character in our story. Forgive us if we have made it all about us. Today we choose to die to ourselves and make our story HISTORY! Let us shine such a bright light everywhere we go that those watching us will see You so clearly, that they will know, it's all about YOU! In Jesus' name, Amen.

What is God speaking to you today?

32. GRACE LIKE A WAVE

John 1:16-17

"And of His fullness we have all received, and grace for grace. For the law was given through Moses, but grace and truth came through Jesus Christ."

THINK ABOUT THAT FOR A MINUTE

The Bible describes grace in various ways, including as a gift, a provision, and a blessing. However, in my opinion, one of the most beautiful illustrations of grace is that of a wave. Just as a wave overwhelms everything in its path, God's grace overflows and covers us completely! Don't you just love that? God's grace is the unmerited favor that God extends to us through the sacrificial death and resurrection of Jesus Christ. Paul refers to grace as a "gift" that is freely given to us. Let's break this down a bit. Look at the nature of a wave. A wave is a powerful force that moves through water or air, carrying energy and momentum. Waves can be gentle or fierce and they can move in a variety of directions. In the same way, God's grace is such a powerful force that moves through our lives, carrying the energy and momentum of His love and forgiveness! Just as a wave can bring calm to a stormy sea,

God's grace can bring peace to our troubled hearts. The source of a wave is often far away from where it eventually breaks on the shore. It may begin as a ripple in the deep ocean, but as it travels closer to land, it gains strength and power. In the same way, God's grace originates from His eternal love and is made manifest through Jesus Christ. It may seem distant at times, but as we draw closer to Him, we experience the fullness of His grace and its transformative power in our lives! Surfers know how to ride the waves, harnessing their power and momentum to move forward. Similarly, we can learn to ride the wave of God's grace by trusting in His love and surrendering to His will. As we do so, we can experience the freedom and joy that come from living in His grace. And just as surfers often share the waves with others, we are called to share the wave of God's grace with those around us. We can do this by extending forgiveness, showing compassion, and sharing the good news of Jesus Christ. When we start to LIVE out this amazing grace, we become vessels of His grace, and others can experience the same transformative power that we have received! That is the ultimate goal! Grace like a wave is a powerful image that illustrates the abundance and generosity of God's grace towards us. It is a gift that we do not deserve, yet it covers all our sins and failures. As believers, we are called to respond to God's grace by living a life that reflects our gratitude and sharing His grace with others.

LET ME CHALLENGE YOU TODAY

Try and remember this throughout the day, that God's grace is like a wave that can transform our lives and the lives of those around us. As we learn to ride this wave, we can experience the fullness of His love and the freedom that comes from living in His grace. We should ALWAYS be mindful of His unmerited favor towards us and seek to extend it to others.

LET ME PRAY FOR YOU TODAY

Jesus, thank You so much for your grace, like a wave! Thank You for covering us so perfectly with 'grace that we never deserved! Help us today to extend Your grace to those around us today. Just as we didn't deserve Your love and grace, let us give as freely as we have received! In Jesus name, Amen.

What is God speaking to you today?

33. POWER IN YOUR WORDS

James 3:5a

""A word out of your mouth may seem of no account, but it can accomplish nearly anything— or destroy it!"

THINK ABOUT THAT FOR A MINUTE

Let me ask you a seemingly hypothetical question... "If every word you spoke came true, would it change the way you speak?" I'll never forget driving to preach at a conference, praying to myself, and I heard God speak to me as clear as day and ask me that very question! I used to do stand-up comedy many years ago. And I was an *insult* comic. I said horrible things to people from the stage. But this also led to me being very sarcastic and hurtful with my words in everyday life as well. After giving my life to Jesus, I changed a LOT! But I was still a bit careless with my words to others and even about myself. Until God asked me that question. So I started to think about it and my answer was, "Yes. If my words ALL came true I would most DEFINITELY start talking differently!" Then God said, "Do that then!" You see, our verse today speaks to the power of our words and the impact they can have, both positively and negatively. As Christians, we are called to use our words to build up, encourage, and spread the love of Christ. However, as

James warns, our tongues can also be incredibly destructive, causing harm and division. Another translation of our verse today says, "the tongue is a small thing that makes grand speeches. But a tiny spark can set a great forest on fire." James compares the tongue to a small spark that can set off a dangerous wildfire. Our words may seem insignificant, but they have the power to ignite conflict, destroy relationships, and cause harm. It's important to recognize the impact our words can have and to use them wisely. James encourages us to "consider" the power of our words. This means taking time to think before we speak and considering the impact our words may have on others. As Christians, we should always strive to speak with love, kindness, and compassion, using our words to build up and encourage those around us. The truth is, WE are made in the image of God! Think about this: how does God create anything? He speaks it into existence! We are the same way. We are building and shaping our world around us with the words we speak! If you don't like the life you have, start speaking differently about it! It sounds crazy, but God's word shows us this is true time and time again. James goes on to say in verses 6-8, that the tongue is also a fire and unlike animals, no man came tame it. These verses emphasize the difficulty of controlling our tongues and the need for God's help to do so. We should pray for wisdom and self-control, asking God to help us use our words for good and to avoid using them for harm. Start thinking of your words as powerful. Because they are! You are building up your-self; your family, your friends, your life *OR* destroying them with every word you speak. I say we speak LIFE today over EVERY-THING! Because you see, it's really not a hypothetical question at all. So I'll leave you with this one more time, "If every word you spoke came true, would it change the way you speak?"

LET ME CHALLENGE YOU TODAY

Take time to reflect on your own words and the impact they have had on those around you. Ask God to help you use your words wisely and to purify your heart, so that your words may reflect the love of Christ. Start building the life you want to see with every word you speak today!

LET ME PRAY FOR YOU TODAY

Father, thank You for making us in Your own image. Thank You for giving us the ability to build and shape the world around us using words the same way you do. Today help us remember how power-ful our words are, so that we can use them to speak life into every person and situation we encounter today. Let us learn to speak like You today Jesus! In Jesus' name, Amen.

What is God speaking to you today?

_____

_____

_____

_____

_____

_____

_____

_____

_____

_____

_____

_____

_____

_____

_____

_____

_____

_____

_____

_____

34. HAPPY HAPPY JOY JOY

Philippians 2:3-4

"Do nothing out of selfish ambition or vain conceit. Rather, in humility value others above yourselves, not looking to your own interests but each of you to the interests of the others."

THINK ABOUT THAT FOR A MINUTE

As humans, we often seek happiness and fulfillment through self-gratification, personal achievement, and material possessions. This is part of our flesh! And the good news is, God understands this! But the Bible teaches us that TRUE happiness comes from serving others and valuing THEIR needs and desires above our own. However, seeking the happiness of others can actually lead to our own happiness! Our verse today begins with the call to do nothing out of selfish ambition or vain conceit. These words remind us that true happiness comes not from personal gain or status but from a humble and selfless attitude. The second part of the passage encourages us to value others above ourselves. This means that we should prioritize the needs and desires of others over our own. It's crazy how backwards this can feel to us sometimes. But that's how almost EVERYTHING in the Word of God works! The truth is however, when we focus on meeting the needs of others, blessing others, and putting them above ourselves, we will actually find our own fulfillment! The reason is, living this way fulfills the will of God in your life! Remember, *to love God and love others*? That's why we find OUR happiness when we focus on the joy of others! That leads to the final phrase of the passage that reminds us exactly that! When we focus on the happiness of others, we will ultimately find our own happiness. This is a powerful reminder that serving others is not just a selfless act, but it also benefits us in the long run. Seeking the happiness of others is a key component of a fulfilling and joyful life. As we practice humility and selflessness, value others above ourselves, and prioritize the needs and desires of those around us, we will find that our own happiness grows and flourishes. Let us strive to live out this truth in our daily lives and encourage others to do the same.

LET ME CHALLENGE YOU TODAY

Take time today to not only focus on what YOU need, but also look for ways to help and be a blessing to those around you. Pay attention to how your mood or attitude shifts as you begin to transform into the hands and feet of Jesus! The joy and fulfillment you get out of meeting others' needs instead of your own is nothing short of incredible! Try it and see!

LET ME PRAY FOR YOU TODAY

Jesus, thank You for being such an amazing example of a servant. May we be more like You today! Help us to put our wants and desires aside and let us see clearly those around us. Let us see people the way YOU see people. So that we can love people the way YOU love people. I thank You for the opportunities even today to be Your hands and feet. Thank You that as we love others, You pour out Your love even greater on us! In Jesus' name, Amen.

What is God speaking to you today?

35. U-N-I-T-WHY?

Genesis 11:6

"Look!" he said. "The people are united, and they all speak the same language. After this, nothing they set out to do will be impossible for them! "

THINK ABOUT THAT FOR A MINUTE

Today's verse comes to us from the story of the "Tower of Babel." God takes a look at this group of unbelievers who have decided to try and make their name great by building a tower to Heaven. That's when God says, because they are UNITED nothing they set out to do will be impossible! Considering the above, how much more so should this statement be true for Christians? If we could just become united, we could accomplish ANYTHING! However, the truth is, as it stands, Christians are probably the most DIVIDED group of people I've ever seen! We've got Baptists, Pentecostals, Episcopalians, Methodist, Wesleyan, Assembly of God . . . are you seeing this? Then on top of the denominations, we can divide Christians even more with little things, like should we celebrate Halloween? Should we sing upbeat praise and worship or hymns? Is Justin Bieber really a Christian or not? Are you seeing how ridiculous this is? It's all just a trap of the devil to keep us DIVIDED! But this is never how God intended it to be. WE are the church! We are NOT a denomination! The problem is, God wants us to be KINGDOM minded, and most Christians are CASTLE minded. Instead of focusing on the entire Kingdom of God, we focus on our one little piece... our castle. Our Church. But the truth is, if we could just find a way to set aside the little differences that DO NOT even matter in the big picture of what God is doing, we would be UNSTOPPABLE! Yes, serve in your church. Care about your church that you attend! But just know that your church is just one small piece in God's Kingdom! It is going to take us all working together to show the lost and broken people of the world what the love of Jesus really looks like, because it doesn't look like division at all. It looks like one big happy family working together to build HIS Kingdom! We should be actively looking for ways to be unified together as believers in Christ. Let's not be "castle minded" anymore! Let's focus on the mighty and wonderful Kingdom of the Lord!

LET ME CHALLENGE YOU TODAY

Being kingdom-minded is essential to living the life God has called us to live. By focusing our hearts and minds on the things of God's kingdom, we can resist temptation, stay focused on what matters, and find purpose in our lives. When we change our mindset, let us also focus on how we can become more unified as the body of Christ. Be intentional today to focus on HIS Kingdom and what it means to be unified in Christ!

LET ME PRAY FOR YOU TODAY

Father, thank You for Your Kingdom! And thank You for our "castles" that You let us be a part of. God, shift our mindset today to become Kingdom-minded. May we focus on You and what You want us to do! Please bring to mind any areas of division and strife we may have allowed in our lives. Show us so that we can give those areas to You. Let us become unstoppable in Kingdom-building *YOUR Kingdom*, because we are a united body! In Jesus' name, Amen.

What is God speaking to you today?

36. JESUS THE CARPENTER

Mark 6:3

"*Then they scoffed, "He's just a carpenter, the son of Mary and the brother of James, Joseph, Judas, and Simon. And his sisters live right here among us." They were deeply offended and refused to believe in him.*"

THINK ABOUT THAT FOR A MINUTE

Today's verse has always been one that blows my mind! Our scripture says that these people were offended and REFUSED to believe in Jesus. Why? Because He was just Mary's son. He was just a carpenter. The people of Nazareth knew Jesus as a carpenter, the son of Mary, and the brother of James, Joseph, Judas, and Simon. Because of this familiarity, they were unable to see Him as anything more. Maybe you're asking right now, "How can this apply to me?" Well, I'm so glad you asked! It is important for us to be aware of our own biases and preconceptions, and to be open to the possibility that God may be working in unexpected ways. I mean, how many times have we only gone to God when we NEED something? Essentially saying, we can build our lives just fine on our own. Until we can't. Until we find ourselves in trouble or in a bind, THEN we go to Jesus. But let me ask you this question, " Who do you think could really build your life better? You? Or a carpenter?" We put so much focus, time and energy into trying to build our lives by ourselves, when Jesus, the creator of the world, who even came in human form as a CARPENTER, obviously knows how to BUILD things better than we do! This verse actually proceeds to say, Jesus could only perform a FEW miracles there because of their unbelief. Listen, don't get in the way of God working on your life because you THINK you can build it better. Trust me, you can't! The Bible says that He is a GOOD Father who takes great care of His children! I promise you that God cares about your life even more than you do. And He has and knows the perfect plan for your life. Trust Him and His process. Let the carpenter build what He's best at. YOU. The rejection of Jesus in Nazareth teaches us about the importance of faith, the danger of unbelief, and the need for humility. By seeking God with an open heart, cultivating faith, and guarding against unbelief, we can recognize Jesus as the Son of God, and we receive the blessings that He has in store for us.

LET ME CHALLENGE YOU TODAY

Don't look to God today just for what you THINK you need or want. Go to Him as the ultimate carpenter who truly knows how to build your life! The carpenter has a vision for the final product before it's ever complete. And Jesus knows what He's doing in you! He is trying to get you to exactly where you need to be, if we just let Him!

LET ME PRAY FOR YOU TODAY

Jesus, thank You for Your perfect plan for our lives. Thank You that just as You created this world so perfectly, You also have plans that are perfect for us. Today we surrender our plans and desires for our lives and we trade them in for Yours. Show us any areas that need adjusting or work inside of us. We invite You to fully access and examine every area of our lives. Build us into the person You have called us to be. In Jesus' name, Amen.

What is God speaking to you today?

_____

_____

_____

_____

_____

_____

_____

_____

_____

_____

_____

_____

_____

_____

_____

_____

_____

_____

_____

_____

_____

37. BLESSED SIN

1 Corinthians 2:9

"That is what the Scriptures mean when they say, "No eye has seen, no ear has heard, and no mind has imagined what God has prepared for those who love him.""

THINK ABOUT THAT FOR A MINUTE

Oh how I love today's verse! This passage should show you that God WANTS to bless you and you can't even imagine how good the blessings are going to be! How amazing is that? It's all because of what a good, good God we serve! However, this is NOT an excuse to call sin a blessing. know what you're thinking right now, "uh.. What do you mean?!" Was I right? Allow me to explain. You can't lie to your boss to get a promotion and then tell everyone, "Look how God has blessed me!" You also can't find a great deal on an amazing new apartment, then move in with your boyfriend/girlfriend and say, "Look how good God is!" if you're not even married but are now living together! Is this making sense? I'm not condemning any lifestyle choices at all right now. I just want you to see how this can easily happen in our lives if we aren't careful. We can actually be sinning and calling it a blessing at the same time. Listen, it's not a blessing if you have to sin to get it. If you have to work to obtain something or accomplish something then you're also going to have to do the work to keep it or sustain it! However, when God blesses you, that comes free and clear! God will maintain what He gives you! Yes, you have to be a good steward of His blessings, but it won't be a constant struggle and worry when His hand is on you. Lastly, this verse is a call to love God. The promise of the things that He has prepared for us is only for those who love Him. This means that we must put God first in our lives, obey His commands, and seek to know Him more deeply. When we do this, we can trust that He will reveal His perfect plan for our lives and guide us every step of the way. We won't have to sin, or force ANYTHING to happen! That's the amazing goodness of the God we GET to serve!

LET ME CHALLENGE YOU TODAY

1 Corinthians 2:9 is a powerful reminder of the wonderful promises that God has in store for those who love Him. Today as we meditate on this verse, let us be reminded of the importance of faith, the limitations of our human understanding, and the call to love God with all our hearts. But let's also make sure that we aren't FORCING blessings that aren't part of God's plan for our lives. Let's trust Him and honor Him in all we do so when we do receive His blessings, we can steward them well, knowing He is going to sustain the gifts He gives!

LET ME PRAY FOR YOU TODAY

Father, thank You that you have amazing blessings in store for us. Blessings we can't even imagine or comprehend. God we ask You to search our hearts and show us any areas in our lives that we have tried to force Your blessing. Show us, so we can repent today. Let us change our minds and change our direction so that we can be in line with You. God, we thank You that when You bring blessings to our lives, we don't have to struggle or strain to keep them, but we do promise to use well that which You have given to us. In Jesus' name, Amen.

What is God speaking to you today?

38. IT'S HARVEST TIME!

Galatians 6:9

"Don't allow yourselves to be weary in planting good seeds, for the season of reaping the wonderful harvest you've planted is coming!"

THINK ABOUT THAT FOR A MINUTE

The book of Galatians, written by the apostle Paul, was written specifically to the churches in the region of Galatia. The main theme of the book is justification by faith, which means that we are saved not by our own works, but by faith in Jesus Christ. Our verse today, found in chapter 6, we find that Paul is giving practical instructions for how to live out our faith in everyday life. This verse is a call to persevere in doing good, even when we face difficulties and opposition. The phrase "doing good" can refer to acts of kindness, generosity, and service to others, as well as living a life of righteousness and obedience to God. The promise of a harvest reminds us that our efforts to do good will be rewarded in due time. This could refer to blessings in this life, but it also points to the ultimate reward of eternal life with God. This verse should be a source of encouragement to you today! YOUR HARVEST IS COMING! If you've been sowing, don't quit! The harvest is on its way! However, I feel like I have to set this straight. Harvest time does NOT mean just sitting back and waiting for "checks in the mail." Ask anyone who has ever grown up on a farm, harvest is the MOST DIFFICULT time of the year! Hence, some of you may have grown tired of sowing good seeds because you haven't seen the harvest you've been expecting. Have you been sowing and you're ready to see your harvest manifest? Sow even more! And understand, I'm not just talking about money here. We often seem to think of sowing just in terms of finances. But God wants you to sow your time, your energy, your love, your life! Do not grow weary in sowing good seeds because your harvest is actually here! It's not about giving a little and then kicking back to relax. It's about giving and then giving some more! Harvest comes at the proper time, not necessarily when we want it or expect it. We should trust in God's timing and keep doing good, even if we don't see immediate results. When you let yourself get caught up in sowing good seeds all day long, it won't take long before your harvest season is happening daily all around you! You won't have to look for it at all. HARVEST TIME IS HERE!

LET ME CHALLENGE YOU TODAY

Today, think of this verse as a powerful reminder to persevere in doing good, trusting in God's timing and focusing on the ultimate reward of eternal life. May we be encouraged by this verse to keep doing what is right and to trust in God's faithfulness and goodness. Look for ways to sow today, then sow some more! Don't grow weary of doing good. Harvest is here!

LET ME PRAY FOR YOU TODAY

Father God, I thank You for this incredible reminder today to not grow weary of doing good. Father, we thank You that You always keep Your promises! So today, start to show us that harvest is here! Give us a new and fresh desire to go and sow seeds with ALL that we have! And as we do, let us realize that the harvest is found in the work that we're doing for You! Give us a new strength today to work YOUR fields with joy and passion! In Jesus' name, Amen.

What is God speaking to you today?

_____

_____

_____

_____

_____

_____

_____

_____

_____

_____

_____

_____

_____

_____

_____

_____

_____

_____

_____

_____

_____

39. THE LORD WITH YOU

Zephaniah 3:17

"The Lord your God is with you, the Mighty Warrior who saves. He will take great delight in you; in his love he will no longer rebuke you, but will rejoice over you with singing."

THINK ABOUT THAT FOR A MINUTE

Zephaniah is a prophet in the Old Testament who prophesied to the people of Judah about the coming day of the Lord. In our verse today, we find a beautiful and comforting message that speaks of the Lord's love and presence among His people. Let's look at the meaning and significance of Zephaniah 3:17 and how it can encourage us in our daily lives. I LOVE that this begins with the words, "The Lord your God is with you." This verse reminds us that the Lord is not distant or uncaring, but rather He is present with His people and takes great delight in them. As Christians, we are called to be joyful and to find our delight in the Lord. This verse reminds us that the Lord rejoices over us with singing and that we should take comfort in His presence and love. But it only gets better from there! This verse also refers to the Lord as the Mighty Warrior who saves. This is a powerful image that reminds us that the Lord is strong and capable of saving us from our enemies, struggles, and pain. We will always face many challenges and struggles in life, but we can take comfort in the knowledge that the Lord is with us and will fight for us. This verse should be a constant reminder to us that the Lord is our protector and defender. But we can't leave out the best part! Our passage also speaks of the Lord's love for His people! It says that he will no longer rebuke us but will love us with His unfailing love. This is a wonderful comfort knowing that no matter what we have done or how we have failed, the Lord loves us unconditionally. As Jesus followers, we are called to love others as Christ has loved us, and this verse reminds us of the depth and breadth of the Lord's love. Zephaniah 3:17 is such a beautiful and comforting message that reminds us of the Lord's love, presence, and strength. As we face challenges and struggles in our lives, may we take comfort in the knowledge that the Lord is with us and will fight for us. May we ALWAYS remember the depth and width of the Lord's love and strive to show that love to others every single day!

LET ME CHALLENGE YOU TODAY

Today, reflect on this beautiful and powerful declaration of God's love and joy for His people. As we reflect on this verse, may we be reminded of the depth of God's love for us and the joy that comes from being in a relationship with Him. Let us seek to live in a way that honors and pleases God today, and EVERYDAY, and may we share the message of His love and joy with others.

LET ME PRAY FOR YOU TODAY

God, we thank You for Your beautiful words to us in Your scriptures! Thank You that You are ALWAYS with us, and there is no one mightier than You! We are honored that You take delight in us! Let us honor You with a life worthy of Your delight. Thank You for always showing us Your unconditional love. Today, help us go out into the world and show that same love to everyone we come into contact with! In Jesus' name, Amen.

What is God speaking to you today?

_____

_____

_____

_____

_____

_____

_____

_____

_____

_____

_____

_____

_____

_____

_____

_____

_____

_____

_____

40. ECHO HIS LOVE

Isaiah 42:12

"Make God's glory resound; echo his praises from coast to coast."

THINK ABOUT THAT FOR A MINUTE

I think it's only fitting that the last devotional of this book be in memory of my mom, *Echo*. She was never a stepmom to me. Since I was a year old, she has loved me as if I were her own. The only reason I am who I am today is because of her. She taught me what it looks like to love God and love people. She was the picture perfect example of the love of Jesus. This devotional is dedicated to her and I'd like to honor her by using her name as the last subject in this book. The concept of an echo is one that is familiar to most of us. It is the reflection of a sound wave off of a surface, producing a repetition of the original sound. In the same way, God's love echoes through our lives, reminding us of His goodness and grace. Let's explore this metaphor further in light of Scripture.1. *Echoes of Creation* (Genesis 1:1-2) In the beginning, God created the heavens and the earth. His voice spoke the world into existence, and His love was evident in every detail of His creation. Just as an echo bounces off a surface, the beauty of creation echoes the majesty of its Creator. When we look at the mountains, the oceans, and the stars, we hear the echoes of God's love for us. 2. *Echoes of Redemption* (Romans 5:8) While we were still sinners, Christ died for us. This sacrificial act echoes the depth of God's love for humanity. Like an echo that resounds long after the original sound, the power of Christ's sacrifice still echoes through time, offering salvation to all who believe. Through Him, we can experience forgiveness, grace, and eternal life. 3. *Echoes of Community* (1 Corinthians '12:12-27) As believers, we are part of the body of Christ. Each one of us has a unique role to play, and together we form a beautiful tapestry of God's love. Just as an echo amplifies the original sound, our collective witness echoes the love of God to the world. When we love and serve one another, we create an echo that resonates far beyond our individual lives. 4. *Echoes of Eternity* (Revelation 21:1-5) One day, God will make all things new. There will be no more tears, no more pain, and no more death. This promise echoes the hope of eternity that we have in Christ. Like an echo that fades into the distance, the struggles of this life will be swallowed up by the glory of God's eternal kingdom. When we fix our eyes on Jesus, we hear the echo of His love calling us home. The metaphor of an echo reminds us that God's love is not a fleeting emotion, but a powerful force that echoes through our lives and through all of creation. As we reflect on the echoes of God's love, may we be inspired to live in such a way that our lives resound with His love and bring glory to His name, *just like my mom did.* She was, is, and forever will be, the greatest Echo of His love there could ever be.

LET ME CHALLENGE YOU TODAY

Today let's look for a way to be an echo of His love! Go out and love someone today that you've never met before. Tell someone about the love of Jesus without using any words. Put your LIFE into it! Be a blessing to strangers, and don't tell a single person! Just cherish in your heart what God is doing through you. This is how my mom, Echo, lived every single day of her life. She honored Jesus with every ounce of her mind, body, and soul. Today, let us all do the same.

LET ME PRAY FOR YOU TODAY

Father, thank You for such an amazing, fulfilling, and perfect love! Thank You for drawing close to us as we've drawn close to You these last 40 days. Give us a fresh fire and passion to be an echo of Your love. Give us the heart to reach YOUR people! Give us a desire to see people come to You through our testimonies. God, we thank You for the gift of Your presence! Now let us go out and shine the light of Your love as bright as possible! In Jesus' name, Amen.

What is God speaking to you today?

_____

_____

_____

_____

_____

_____

_____

_____

_____

_____

_____

_____

_____

_____

_____

_____

_____

_____

_____

_____

ABOUT THE AUTHOR

Kelly K is a Husband, Father of five, Preacher, Teacher, Writer and Motivational Speaker. Preaching the love of Jesus in a manner that is both progressive and passionate. Kelly K is a highly sought-after conference speaker, and social media Evangelism teacher. His messages reach out to inspire and encourage millions of lives through many multimedia platforms.

Kelly K's approach to speaking focuses on bridging the gap of cultures, ages, and society by offering a sound that is relative to every listener. His message is one of love, faith, joy and hope in Jesus Christ. Kelly K travels to any distance to share this amazing reckless love of Jesus and offer a new perspective on how to reach a world that is used to tuning out anything even slightly, "religious". So many have been blessed by the words, love and passion of Kelly K.

Kelly K currently lives in Kingfisher, Oklahoma with his beautiful wife Lindsay, and his five children, Brennen, Chase, Jaxx, and Jett. He is currently the Associate Pastor at Limitless Church of Kingfisher

CONNECT WITH ME

FOLLOW KELLY K ON SOCIAL MEDIA FOR DAILY POSTS,

VIDEOS, SERMONS, BIBLE STUDIES, AND MORE!

 @KellyKMinistries

 Facebook.com/TheKellyK

 @KellyK_13

 YouTube.com/KellyKMinistry

www.KellyKMinstries.com

TO REQUEST KELLY K TO COME AND SPEAK AT YOUR CHURCH OR

EVENT, PLEASE EMAIL:

KELLYKOPP@GMAIL.COM

To support this ministry:

 @KELLYK13 $KELLYKOPP13